Rediscovering the Jewish Holidays

Tradition in a Modern Voice

Nina Beth Cardin

Behrman House, Inc.

"Adonai spoke to Moses: . . . I have filled [Bezalel] with a divine spirit of skill, ability, and knowledge in every kind of artistic work: to make designs for work in gold, silver, and copper, to cut stones for setting and to carve wood, and to work in every kind of craft" (Exodus 31:3–5).

This book is dedicated to the daughters of Bezalel, whose artistry, skill, ability, and knowledge fill the pages of this book with a divine spirit and beauty.

—N.B.C. and G.G.

The publisher gratefully acknowledges the cooperation of the following sources of photographs and graphic images:

Albatros/Israel Ministry of Tourism 20; **Kathy Bloomfield** 34, 130; **Creative Image Photography** 7, 12–13, 26, 29 (bottom), 32–33, 35, 52–53, 58, 62, 69, 71, 73, 75, 77, 84, 98–100, 102, 118, 124, 128 (bottom), 135, 143, 150, 177, 179, 181 (bottom), 193; **Gustav Doré** 42, 47 (center), 93, 119, 159 (center), 182; **John Reed Forsman/HUC Skirball Cultural Center, Museum Collection** 175 (center); **Gila Gevirtz** 19, 22–23, 37, 59, 68, 87, 104–105, 107, 113, 123, 146–147, 152, 156 (top center), 162, 166, 167 (two at top), 191; **Itamar Grinberg/Israeli Ministry of Tourism** 114; **David Hollander/Congregation B'nai Jeshurun, Short Hills, NJ** 183 (bottom); **Doron Horowitz (ERETZ)/Ministry of Tourism** 167 (bottom); **Israel Information Center** 168; **Israel Ministry of Tourism** 167 (second from bottom), 195; **Jewish National Fund** 110; **Terry Kaye** 8, 21; **Francene Keery** 46–47, 90–91, 96, 101, 121; **Richard Lobell** 6, 9–11, 16–17, 24, 27, 49, 60–61, 66–67, 72, 76, 116–117, 126–127, 133, 136–142, 153, 181 (top), 192; **Museum of Jewish Heritage** 148 (top); **Beth Shepherd Peters** 40, 188; **Sheila Plotkin** 18; **Clare Sieffert** 122; **SPL/Photo Researchers** 80–81; **Ginny Twersky** 38, 44, 56–57, 64, 132; **Therese Wagner** 190; **Beverly Weiss** 54; **Sunny Yellen** 164; **Zionist Archives** 163

Torah Mantle, page 175 (center): Maker: Peachy Levy, Santa Monica, 1991; wool, embroidered and appliquéd with cotton and metallic thread; Museum commission; HUCSM 60.138

Published by Behrman House, Inc.
Springfield, NJ 07081
www.behrmanhouse.com

Library of Congress Cataloging-in-Publication Data

Cardin, Nina Beth
    Rediscovering the Jewish holidays: tradition in a modern voice / Nina Beth Cardin with Gila Gevirtz
        p. cm.
    Includes index.
    ISBN 0-87441-663   9
    1. Fasts and feasts—Judaism—Juvenile literature. 2. Jewish religious education—Textbooks for children. I. Gevirtz, Gila. II. Title.

BM690.C35 2002
296.4'3—dc21

2001056622

Manufactured in the United States of America

Contents

CHAPTER 1

An Open Invitation

"Celebration" by Lydie Egosi

You've been invited to share in the treasures of Jewish tradition and—as importantly—to contribute to them; to pass on the traditions that came before us and also to enrich them for those who will come after us. In fact, you probably have accepted this invitation many times and in many different ways, whether you were aware of it or not.

Each time you tell the story of the Exodus at Passover or a story from your own experience, you share in our tradition *and* you enrich it. When you read from the High Holiday prayer book or when you recite your own prayers, you do the same. And each time you attend a bar or bat mitzvah celebration and observe rituals passed on by others, such as listening to a *d'var Torah,* or when you add a personal touch, perhaps by asking an interesting question, you honor and contribute to the treasures of our people.

As a partner in the *Brit,* the Jewish people's Covenant with God, the invitation is your birthright, available to you on any day at any hour, holy day or weekday, with your family or community, or privately by yourself. At any of these times and in any of these ways—whenever you accept the invitation—*your* ideas, *your* experiences, and *your* sacred acts contribute to the knowledge, the strength, and the purpose of our people.

In return, you are asked to extend this same invitation to others: those who are members of synagogues and those who are not; those who were born Jewish and those who chose to be Jewish; those who agree with you and those who do not. You are asked to be welcoming and open to every Jew who seeks to add to the blessings of our people and to the goodness of the world.

It All Began at Sinai

The ancient rabbis teach us that every Jewish soul was present at Mount Sinai when the Torah was given by God to the Jewish people. They also taught that God gave the Torah to the community as a whole *and simultaneously* to each of us individually, according to our abilities and needs.

When we study Torah together—rabbis, teachers, students, and families in synagogues, schools, and homes—it is as if we are helping one another remember what we heard. When we study together, we can contribute our ideas to the community and learn from the wisdom of others. We have the opportunity to raise new questions as well as share new understandings. This is our tradition.

Although the *text* of the Torah—every single letter—remains the same, our *understanding* of the Torah changes in every generation. It *must* if we are to fulfill the *Brit,* our agreement to live as a holy people by performing mitzvot, such as giving tzedakah, observing Shabbat and holidays, and pursuing peace and justice. If our understandings do not change, how can we perform mitzvot in a way that makes sense for our times?

For example, in ancient Israel helping the needy meant helping to house, feed, and clothe neighbors, or perhaps a poor family one or two villages away. In contrast, modern communication and transportation—telephones, computers, automobiles, and jets—make the opportunity and obligation to give tzedakah much broader. We now must consider the needs of strangers who live far from us, as well as those of our next door neighbors.

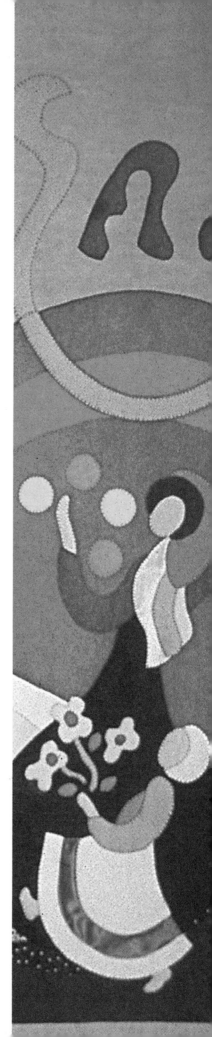

MAKING YOUR CONTRIBUTIONS

Describe a time when you contributed to Jewish tradition through your participation in a holiday or life-cycle celebration.

_____

_____

_____

_____

How does it make you feel to know that you can not only observe and pass on Jewish traditions but also help create and enrich them? Why?

_____

_____

_____

_____

In what ways can a Passover seder be enriched by the questions participants ask and the ideas and experiences they share?

Similarly, because our ancestors did not have electricity and the inventions that use it, they could not tell us how appliances—for example, DVD players, fax machines, and electronic keyboards—can or cannot be used to perform the mitzvot of celebrating Purim, visiting the sick, or leading a prayer service. Instead, *we* must figure this out. Our modern community of Jews, having studied the wisdom of those who came before us, must arrive at new understandings and customs for our times.

Our Ancient Tradition Inspires Creativity

Often it is our ancient tradition itself that inspires us to develop new customs and rituals. Nowhere is this more evident than in our holiday celebrations. Just as the Bible instructs us to make time holy by coming together as families and communities on

One reason the ancient rabbis offer for why there are no vowels in the Torah is that while the consonants remain the same—uniting Jews throughout time—each generation must supply its own vowels, to speak the Torah in its own voice.

Making Modern Technologies into Mitzvah Technologies

How can a car be turned into a "mitzvah mobile" in response to famine or earthquake victims?

_____

_____

How can a telephone, fax machine, or computer help you perform the mitzvah of *bikkur ḥolim*—visiting the sick—when you live far from the person who is ill?

_____

_____

How can a computer be used to perform the mitzvah of rodef shalom—*pursuing peace? What other mitzvot can be performed using a computer?*

Rosh Hashanah, Yom Kippur, Passover, Shavuot, and Sukkot, so, many generations after Sinai, these traditions inspired our people to make time holy by establishing the newer holidays and customs of Ḥanukkah, Purim, Tu B'Shevat, and Yom Ha'atzma'ut.

Just as our ancient sages created prayers from biblical texts and from the poetry of their souls—giving us the Sh'ma, from the Book of Deuteronomy, and the Amidah, which is part of every prayer service—so, too, modern Jews have created prayers for the new holidays of Yom Hashoah and Yom Yerushalayim, as well as for life-cycle events such as weddings and baby namings. And just as the sages created a Haggadah to help sanctify Passover, so, too, in November 2001 did American Jews build on Jewish tradition by creating Haggadot [plural of Haggadah] to help sanctify the secular holiday of Thanksgiving. These Haggadot include rituals and prayers to express grief over the September 11 attack on the United States, gratitude for the freedom and bounty of America, and hope for a better future.

Not only does each genera-tion add its understanding and traditions to the treasury of Jewish life, but the diverse com-munities of the Jewish people also enrich Judaism. As you read *Rediscovering the Jewish Holidays: Tradition in a Modern Voice,* you will learn about different customs that are observed by Reform, Reconstructionist, Conservative, and Orthodox Jews, and about special traditions that are observed by Jews from distant lands, such as Turkey, Russia, Italy, and Poland. You will learn that although we are one people, we have many different customs. And you will learn that you are valued as much for developing and sharing your ideas as you are for studying and observing our ancient traditions.

As you read Rediscovering the Jewish Holidays, *you will learn that even a simple ritual, such as dipping one's finger into the Passover wine as the names of the plagues are recited, may be performed in many different ways.*

Participate in the Challenge

Rediscovering the Jewish Holidays is filled with the creative challenge of being Jewish. It will deepen your understanding of Jewish life and values, and help you enrich our tradition. You will be encouraged to make personal contributions, such as adding beauty and meaning to holidays through *hiddur mitzvah,* the beautification of mitzvot. *Hiddur mitzvah* includes the many ways Jewish observance can be made more sacred through artistic touches, such as placing a ceramic or silver Kiddush cup on a Shabbat or holiday table, using a finely crafted *ḥanukkiyah* to hold Ḥanukkah candles, and hanging festive sukkah decorations to celebrate the autumn harvest.

What Do You Think?

Why do you think our tradition encourages us to enrich our holiday and ritual observance with beautiful objects, special songs, and delicious foods?

_____

_____

_____

_____

How do the choices we make also help us personalize the holidays?

_____

_____

_____

_____

As you read this book, your deepening understanding of the holidays may influence choices you make in your daily life. For example, after reflecting on the High Holiday tradition of giving tzedakah, you may be inspired to help those in need on a more regular basis; and upon considering the custom of bringing

שבת

A beautiful ḥallah cover can add joy to a Friday night meal and personalize the sacred act of observing Shabbat.

mishloaḥ-manot—hamantashen and other sweets—to friends and family on Purim, you may be motivated to become a more giving son or daughter, sister or brother, or friend.

"Let the old become new and the new become holy." So said Rav Abraham Kook, the first Ashkenazic (eastern European) chief rabbi of modern Israel. Let us now explore how, in our generation, each of us can renew and add holiness to Jewish tradition.

CHAPTER 2

THE JEWISH CALENDAR
Making Time Holy

Without a calendar, how would we know when to show up for holidays such as Ḥanukkah—for lighting candles, playing dreidel, opening gifts, and noshing on potato latkes and jelly doughnuts?

Calendars not only help us name time—the days of the week, the months, and the years—they also help us mark time as individuals and as a community. They help us agree on what day today is, when the World Series will be played, how old we are, when the school year begins, and when summer vacation will end.

Throughout history, there have been hundreds of different calendars, each one reflecting the stories and values of the people who created it. For example, in ancient times, the days of the week were each dedicated to a god or goddess. As a result, in many languages, they are named after deities. Thursday, for instance, is named for the Teutonic god Thor (Thor's day), and Saturday is named for the Roman god Saturn (Saturn's day). Today the world shares one global calendar—the Gregorian, or civil, calendar set by Pope Gregory XIII in 1582. Yet as Jews, we also continue to mark time according to our own traditions and calculations.

The Gregorian calendar begins with January 1 and ends with December 31. It is a solar calendar; that is, it is based on the *earth's rotation around the sun.* That journey, as you know, takes

THE DAYS OF CREATION

יוֹם אֶחָד	Day 1	Creation of light
יוֹם שֵׁנִי	Day 2	Creation of heaven and earth
יוֹם שְׁלִישִׁי	Day 3	Creation of dry land and sea, grass, vegetation, and fruit trees
יוֹם רְבִיעִי	Day 4	Creation of the sun and the moon
יוֹם חֲמִישִׁי	Day 5	Creation of fish and birds
יוֹם הַשִּׁשִּׁי	Day 6	Creation of bugs, land animals, and humans
יוֹם הַשְּׁבִיעִי	Day 7	Shabbat, day of rest

The first commandment given to the Jewish people when they left Egypt was:

הַחֹדֶשׁ הַזֶּה לָכֶם רֹאשׁ חֳדָשִׁים...

This month shall be for you the beginning of months . . . (Exodus 12:2).

Of all the laws that would be given to the Jews, why start with that law? Because freedom means being in charge of your time, organizing it as it suits you, naming it as you want to, and creating the sacred days that honor the precious memories and events of your life. After the Exodus, the Israelites' time was no longer Egyptian time. The Israelites' new lives required a new calendar, one that reflected their relationship with God, and identified holy time.

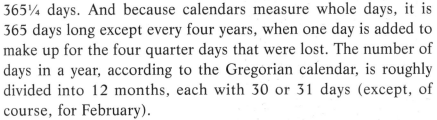

Counting the Days

According to the Gregorian calendar, days begin at midnight. In contrast, the Bible teaches that days begin at sunset. As it says in the story of Creation in Genesis, "And there was evening, and there was morning, a first day." This is why the celebration of most Jewish holidays begins at sunset. (The rituals of minor fast days, such as the 17th of Tammuz, begin at dawn.)

365¼ days. And because calendars measure whole days, it is 365 days long except every four years, when one day is added to make up for the four quarter days that were lost. The number of days in a year, according to the Gregorian calendar, is roughly divided into 12 months, each with 30 or 31 days (except, of course, for February).

The Jewish, or Hebrew, calendar is a lunar calendar and was created more than *2,000* years ago. It is based on the *moon's rotation around the earth,* which takes 29½ days. So a Jewish month is counted as either 29 or 30 days. Twelve of these months make one year.

But now a problem arises. Twelve lunar months add up to approximately 354 days—11 days short of a solar year. If we didn't adjust the Jewish calendar to match the solar year, each Jewish year would be 11 days shorter than a full trip by the earth around the sun. That would cause Rosh Hashanah—and all the other Jewish holidays—to arrive 11 days earlier each year on the solar calendar, and the seasons would wander around the year, first 11 days too "early," then 22 days, then 33, and so on. Soon, for example, Rosh Hashanah would be in the summer, and then in the spring. After a while, Ḥanukkah would fall during summer vacation. This would be especially awkward for the three harvest holidays—Passover, Shavuot, and Sukkot—that are tied to the seasons of the Land of Israel. It would not do to celebrate Sukkot, the fall harvest, in early spring!

To solve the problem, the lunar calendar must occasionally be adjusted, just as the solar calendar is by the leap year. But, instead of adding one *day* in its leap year, the Jewish calendar adds a whole *month*. The regular Jewish year is divided into 12 months: Tishre, Ḥeshvan, Kislev, Tevet, Shevat, Adar, Nisan, Iyar, Sivan, Tammuz, Av, and Elul. The additional month that is added on leap years is called Adar Bet (or Adar Sheni)—Adar 2 (or the second Adar)—for it is inserted after the regular late-winter month of Adar.

The Jewish leap year occurs more often than the solar year's: It must come seven times within a 19-year cycle to align regularly with the solar calendar. That averages out to one leap year every two or three years. Whereas in any given year the lunar calendar will be either a bit longer or a bit shorter than the solar calendar (which is why we say the holidays are either "early" or "late"), everything evens out within a year or two.

As you read this book you will learn why and how we observe the holidays that come in each season of the Jewish year. You will discover how our traditions enrich and strengthen us as individuals, as families, and as a community. And you will learn how to honor *and* add to our tradition of making time holy.

Festival Dates

In biblical times, when the new moon was seen in Jerusalem, a new month—Rosh Ḥodesh—was proclaimed. Special fires were lit all over Israel to announce the new month. But it took longer for the news to reach Jews living outside of Israel. Concerned that they might begin the month on the wrong day, and thus also celebrate holidays on the wrong day, they added an extra day of celebration to the three festivals on which pilgrimages were made to Jerusalem: Passover, Shavuot, and Sukkot. This way they were confident that one of the days had to be right. This is a tradition that Orthodox and Conservative Jews living outside of Israel continue to this day.

This wall hanging, "Arizona Sunset," is by Judaic artist Sheila Groman. Whether in Arizona, the Amazon, or the Alps, for the Jewish people sunset signals the beginning of a day.

CHAPTER 3

רֹאשׁ הַשָּׁנָה

ROSH HASHANAH
Cleaning the Slate

1–2 Tishre

Today is the birthday of the world.
—from the High Holiday prayer book

Like footprints that are the telltale signs of a person we do not see, each of nature's wonders reminds us that God is present in the world.

The Book of Genesis tells us that God, after working for six days, completing the heavens and the earth and all that was in them, looked at the brand new world and declared, "It is very good." The Torah's words can be understood as both a prayer *and* a sacred teaching: This world may not be perfect, but it has infinite value. Though it was born with blemishes and shortcomings, do not forget that it can be very good. It is your responsibility to find the good and help it grow.

And so, Rosh Hashanah, the Jewish New Year, is not only our annual celebration of the birth of the world, it is also the holiday on which we renew our commitment to see and nurture the goodness in ourselves and in the rest of Creation. It is the sacred time our tradition gives us to acknowledge our achievements and regret our mistakes, to express gratitude for the good in our lives and extend our apologies to those we have hurt, and to forgive ourselves for our imperfections and accept our limitations.

Seeing Our Goodness

On Rosh Hashanah our prayers speak of God as Judge and Ruler. They imagine a divine court in which God sits on the throne of justice reviewing our deeds. On a table before God lies a large book with many pages, as many as there are people in the world. Each of us has our own page. Written on it, in our own hand, are all our actions of the past year. Our tradition teaches that God considers what we have done and weighs the good against the bad.

In order to make sense out of death and the bad things that happen to people, many Jews came to believe that misfortune and death were punishments for sin. And so our ancient prayers declare that God judges us and then decides "who shall live and who shall die." But, according to the ancient sages, the purpose of God's judgments is not to punish us but instead to explore the goodness that is inside each of us, and to help it grow.

Self-Assessment

It is not only God who judges us. In private moments we often judge ourselves: when we lie in bed at night, when we take walks alone, when we sit quietly by ourselves. It is good to use such opportunities to make an honest assessment of how well we live our lives, how well we nurture the goodness in ourselves, and how we can improve.

Have you ever felt unworthy after making a mistake, a "bad move"? If you have, then you haven't been fair to yourself. Just as succeeding at something doesn't mean that everything about you is perfect, making a mistake only means that you are human.

What Do You Think?
Describe one benefit of setting aside a time each year when the community comes together to review the past year and to pray for the strength to do even better in the coming year.

MISTAKES ARE PART OF THE GAME

Francis T. Vincent, Jr., former commissioner of baseball, could have been giving a High Holiday sermon when he said, "Baseball teaches us how to deal with failure, that failure is the norm in baseball—that those who hit safely in one out of three chances become star players. . . . Baseball . . . considers errors to be part of the game, part of its rigorous truth."

How can acknowledging mistakes help an athlete improve?

_____

_____

_____

How can acknowledging our weaknesses as well as our strengths on Rosh Hashanah help us become better people?

_____

_____

_____

BECOMING THE BEST YOU CAN BE

One important lesson of Rosh Hashanah is that although none of us is perfect, each of us has great potential for goodness. All that is required of us is to be our best selves. Rabbi Zusya, an 18th century Ḥasid, said, "In the world to come, they will not ask me, 'Why were you not Moses?' They will ask me, 'Why were you not Zusya?'"

Describe one action you took last year that helped you grow goodness inside you, for example, a time when you showed concern or respect for others.

_____

_____

Describe one goal you have for the new year that will help you grow the goodness inside you so that you can become your best self.

_____

_____

During the weeks before Rosh Hashanah, we greet one another and send cards with this wish: לְשָׁנָה טוֹבָה תִּכָּתֵבוּ *(May you be inscribed in the Book of Life for a good year). Between Rosh Hashanah and Yom Kippur, we make this wish:* גְּמַר חֲתִימָה טוֹבָה *(May you be sealed in the Book of Life).*

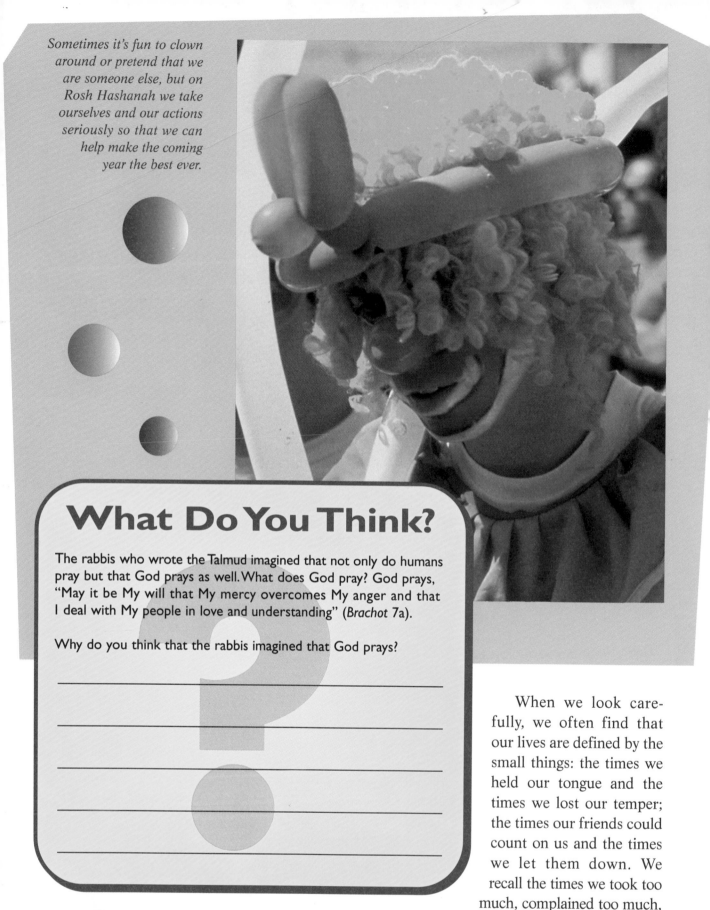

Sometimes it's fun to clown around or pretend that we are someone else, but on Rosh Hashanah we take ourselves and our actions seriously so that we can help make the coming year the best ever.

What Do You Think?

The rabbis who wrote the Talmud imagined that not only do humans pray but that God prays as well. What does God pray? God prays, "May it be My will that My mercy overcomes My anger and that I deal with My people in love and understanding" (*Brachot* 7a).

Why do you think that the rabbis imagined that God prays?

_____

_____

_____

_____

_____

When we look carefully, we often find that our lives are defined by the small things: the times we held our tongue and the times we lost our temper; the times our friends could count on us and the times we let them down. We recall the times we took too much, complained too much, spent too much, and cared too little; the times we were silent when we should have spoken up, and the times we spoke up when it would have been kinder to be silent.

Rosh Hashanah is a day set aside for such remembering. (In fact, another name for the holiday is *Yom Hazikaron* which means "the Day of Remembering.") On Rosh Hashanah we ask both God and ourselves to see our goodness, understand our weaknesses, accept our regrets, deepen our wisdom, and strengthen our determination to help goodness flourish inside us.

We also ask God to pardon us when our offense is against both God and another person. What is an offense against God? Is it when we reject God's rituals, for example, by not lighting Shabbat or holiday candles? Yes, for it is as if we reject a gift. But it is also when we reject God's ways. For our tradition teaches, "What is good and what is it that God wants of you but to do justly, pursue kindness, and walk humbly with your God" (Micah 6:8).

When we fail to live as God's partners—which we all do at times— we can seek *God's* forgiveness. But when we hurt other people, we must first ask for *their* forgiveness. God can forgive us only after we have sought the forgiveness of those we have wronged.

This boy is looking forward to the holiday meal that he is helping his grandmother prepare. How is he fulfilling Micah's description of what is good, and what God wants of us?

Below are two columns labeled for the two categories of offenses for which we ask for forgiveness. In each column, one example is listed. Add three additional examples.

OFFENSES AGAINST GOD	OFFENSES AGAINST OTHER PEOPLE
1. eating bread on Passover	1. gossiping
2. _____	2. _____
3. _____	3. _____
4. _____	4. _____

Preparing for Rosh Hashanah: The Month of Elul

Certainly we can ask forgiveness at any time of the year. But the month before Rosh Hashanah, the month of Elul, is an especially good time. It is not always easy to approach someone and say, "If I have hurt you this past year, I am sorry. Please forgive me." Elul, the month of repairing relationships, gives us the encouragement and the opportunity to do so.

Some people seek forgiveness face-to-face. Some find it easier to write a letter. Others may want to offer a gift or do a favor as part of making apologies and amends. Asking forgiveness may take many forms. But the one common element is that the apology must be clearly stated to the one we have wronged.

During Elul we not only ask others to pardon us, we also are asked to pardon others. Sometimes it is easy to forgive the small wrongs unintentionally committed. But at other times, it is hard. How can we forgive others after cruel words or spiteful acts have shamed or hurt us? How can we be certain that others are truly sorry, that they have earned our forgiveness, that they deserve such kindness from us?

Rosh Hashanah teaches us that just as we ask God to trust that we are worthy of forgiveness, so we must be open to others who seek our forgiveness.

The Three Steps to Forgiveness

How can we earn the forgiveness of others? How can we learn to forgive ourselves? And, if anger, hurt, or resentment keep us from regretting our actions, how can we begin to soften our hearts?

The prayers of Rosh Hashanah present three steps: *teshuvah* (acts of repentance), *tefillah* (prayer), and *tzedakah* (giving to those in need).

Teshuvah

Teshuvah means "returning." It means realizing that we are not stuck but rather that we can turn around and correct our mistakes. The process of *teshuvah* begins when we acknowledge that what we did was wrong. It continues when we ask for forgiveness from the person we wronged (including ourselves) and when we strive not to do it again.

There are times, however, when we may feel so angry, so hurt, or so guilty that we cannot bring ourselves to apologize. Then the question is, How do we do *teshuvah*? The answer is, When our hearts are not in it, we start with simple acts of *teshuvah*. We go through the motions, not to fool the other person, but rather to open ourselves to the feelings of *teshuvah*. Just as the act of dressing up can help us feel elegant or festive, so too the act of repentance can help us feel regret.

Tefillah

The holiday prayers found in the *maḥzor*, the special prayer book created for Rosh Hashanah and Yom Kippur, speak of God's goodness and righteousness, of how God cares for us—all of us—and seeks our return to holy ways.

Wronging Ourselves

Sometimes we wrong ourselves, for example, when we ride a bike without wearing a helmet, are hypercritical of our actions, or eat unhealthfully a lot. We also wrong ourselves when we ignore opportunities to grow the good inside us. When this happens, we may have to ask for forgiveness from ourselves as well as from another person.

How have you wronged yourself during this past year? How can you develop the willingness to both forgive yourself and try to do better next year?

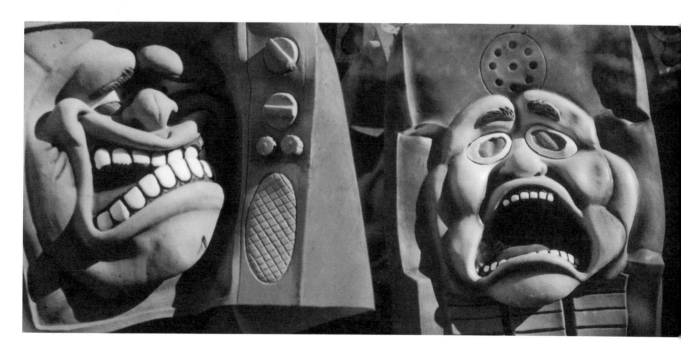

Sometimes anger can be a mask that hides our hurt feelings. How can offering an apology, or accepting someone else's words of regret, become a way to acknowledge our hurt, or to heal an emotional wound?

Sometimes as we pray, we want to say things not found in the prayer book. Sometimes we want to pray directly from our hearts. On Rosh Hashanah, we are encouraged to pray using both the words of the *maḥzor* and the words from our hearts.

Tzedakah

Judaism teaches that every person is made in the image of God—*b'tzelem Elohim.* Judaism also teaches that every person has the right to a life of dignity as well as the obligation to treat others with dignity. Giving tzedakah—gifts of money, food, warm clothing, talents, and time—is one way each of us can meet that obligation.

Tzedakah is not a penalty for wrongdoing or a fine, a bribe, or a bargaining chip. Rather, tzedakah is a mitzvah, a holy act that

TAKING ACTION: TZEDAKAH

On Rosh Hashanah we are reminded that no matter what mistakes we have made, we can always begin the process of returning to God's path of goodness and mercy through the mitzvah of tzedakah.

How can you fulfill the mitzvah of tzedakah in honor of Rosh Hashanah?

_____

_____

How can this act of tzedakah help return some of the goodness that might have been lost from the world during the past year?

_____

_____

What can you do to make tzedakah a habit, a daily or weekly reminder that every person—young or old, rich or poor, educated or unschooled—is responsible for contributing goodness and justice to the world?

_____

_____

The word tzedakah *comes from the same root as the word* tzedek, *meaning "justice." How can helping those in need add justice to the world?*

Rabbi Irwin Kula teaches that during the Ten Days of Repentance, one way in which we can evaluate how we are living our lives is to look at how we are spending our money. How much money has been spent on entertainment? tzedakah? food? clothing? gifts for others? What does this tell us about what and who we value? love? honor? respect?

Keep a record of how you spend your money, be it allowance, gift money, or money earned from babysitting and other jobs. (See the sample form below.) Alone or with your family, look through your records carefully and discover what they reveal about you.

SAMPLE EXPENSE FORM	
ITEM	**AMOUNT**
_____	_____
_____	_____
_____	_____
_____	_____
_____	_____
Tzedakah	_____
Savings	_____
TOTAL	_____

In response to what you discover, consider how changing your spending habits can help you become the best person you can be. A financial accounting, *heshbon mamonim,* can lead you toward a spiritual accounting, *heshbon hanefesh.*

gives back to the world some of the goodness we may have removed in moments of weakness or self-centeredness. It reminds us that our own fortune is tied to the fortunes of all people, to the fortunes of all Creation.

How We Celebrate

The season of the New Year begins 30 days before Rosh Hashanah, on Rosh Hodesh Elul, the first day of the month of Elul. From that day until the day before Rosh Hashanah, the hollowed-out ram's horn known as the shofar is blown every morning in synagogue. In ancient times, the shofar was used for many reasons, including to announce the new month, to alert the Israelites to danger, and to assemble them for war. Today the shofar is commonly used to declare that Rosh Hashanah—the Day of Judgment—is approaching.

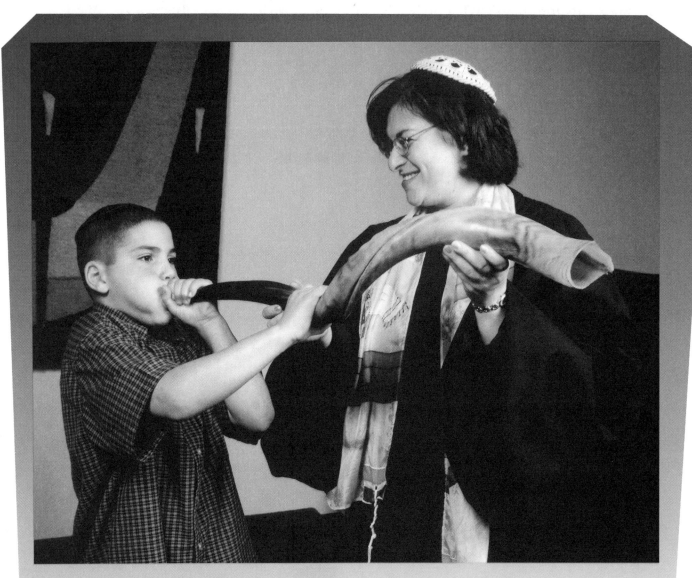

One way to prepare for Rosh Hashanah is to learn how to blow a shofar so that you can help out at synagogue services.

Beginning with the last week of Elul, additional prayers called Seliḥot are added to the morning service. Seliḥot are prayers that speak of our sorrow for whatever wrongs we have done. Seliḥot is also the name of the midnight service held at many synagogues, usually on the Saturday night before Rosh Hashanah. Some synagogues turn the evening into a community event, with special activities for adults, children, teens, and families.

Light Bulbs: Sharing Your Bright Ideas

Imagine that you are a member of your synagogue's ritual committee, which helps make decisions on religious observance. Write a memo describing what you want to include in the community Seliḥot event to attract teens and help get them into the spirit of the High Holidays. Explain why you think your ideas would work.

_____

_____

_____

_____

_____

_____

_____

_____

The Bible (Leviticus 23:24) tells us to observe the first day of Tishre as a holy day. But for the same reason that a day was added to the pilgrimage holidays (see "Festival Dates" on page 15), a second day was added to Rosh Hashanah. This second day is celebrated by Jews in Israel as well as by a large number of Jews outside of Israel. However, many Reform congregations continue the biblical practice of observing only one day.

On Rosh Hashanah, we eat special foods. Ḥallah— the sweet, golden, braided bread we eat on Shabbat and holidays—is now round instead of long, resembling a regal crown and reminding us that God is our Ruler. Apples are dipped in honey to symbolize the sweet year that we hope lies ahead.

Honey, apples, and round ḥallah—often with raisins—are tasty symbols of the goodness and pleasure we hope will be ours in the coming year.

ONE PEOPLE, MANY CUSTOMS:
A Rosh Hashanah Seder

Passover is not the only holiday with a seder, or ritual meal. Traditionally, Sephardic Jews (Jews coming largely from Portugal and the Mediterranean countries) enrich their Rosh Hashanah meal with a modest New Year's seder. They set out plates with special foods that—because of a play on words or a folk belief associated with them—symbolize health, long life, abundance, or security. An appropriate prayer is recited before each food is eaten. For example, *karah* is a squash, and the word sounds like the Hebrew word for "undoing." So as the squash is eaten, the participants say, "Undo our harsh sentence, and remember our merits."

North American Jews continue a hint of this tradition when we dip the apple in honey and say, "May this coming year be a year of sweetness and goodness for us, Israel, and all the inhabitants of the earth."

You can create your own Rosh Hashanah seder and rituals for the first night of the holiday. For example, round objects (such as the High Holiday hallah) can symbolize life; pomegranates can symbolize love and abundance; olives can symbolize peace. Feel free to make your own food selections and to create your own accompanying prayers (keeping them to one line is usually appreciated). Invite guests to bring a special food and offer their own wishes.

List one symbolic food that you can add to your holiday menu, and write a prayer that can be recited before eating it.

_____

_____

_____

_____

It is customary to wear new clothes on the second day of Rosh Hashanah and to eat a fruit we have not eaten in a long time.

Prayer services are held in synagogue starting on the eve of Rosh Hashanah. The most familiar sound of the Rosh Hashanah service is the shofar. It is blown 100 times in the synagogue on each of the two days. These 100 blasts are made up of three different voices: *tekiah*, or one long blast; *shvarim*, a series of three medium blasts; and *truah*, a series of nine short blasts. Some imagine the shofar's sound as an urgent call for help

ברוך אתה יי אלהינו מלך העולם

שהחינו

וקימנו והגיענו לזמן הזה

On Rosh Hashanah, as on other holidays, we recite the Sheheḥeyanu blessing. This wall hanging by Peachy Levy has the Hebrew words without vowels. Can you read the blessing?

In ancient Israel, on sacred occasions a shofar was blown, trumpets were played, and vocal music was sung by singers in the Temple. Today, some synagogues permit music to be played on holy days, such as Rosh Hashanah, while others do not. Although we are one people, we have many different customs.

(*tekiah*), the sound of protest or pain (*shvarim*), and the sound of sobbing (*truah*). It is as if the shofar becomes our throats and our mouths, crying out for us in a way that we may feel too proud or filled with decorum to do.

Back to the Sources

On Rosh Hashanah the Torah reading includes verses from Genesis 24 and Numbers 29. Numbers 29:1 instructs us to hold a holy gathering on the first day of Tishre:

...מִקְרָא־קֹדֶשׁ יִהְיֶה לָכֶם כָּל־מְלֶאכֶת עֲבֹדָה לֹא תַעֲשׂוּ

יוֹם תְּרוּעָה יִהְיֶה לָכֶם:

. . . You shall have a holy gathering; you shall do no servile work. It shall be your day of sounding the shofar.

Emptying Ourselves of Wrongdoings

On the afternoon of the first day of Rosh Hashanah (or the second day if the first day is Shabbat), Jews perform the symbolic ritual of *tashlich* (meaning to "throw or cast off"). The ritual was inspired by a verse from the prophet Micah: "God will take us back in love; God will defeat our wickedness and cast our sins into the depths of the sea" (7:19). We go alone or as a community to the shores of a lake, stream, or reservoir; there, we recite psalms of compassion and forgiveness. Then, using stones or bread to represent our sins, we throw these "sins" into the water. *Tashlich* might not literally relieve us of our sins. Yet somehow we may feel lighter on the way home.

Days of Awe

Aseret Y'mei Teshuvah (the Ten Days of Repentance) is one name for the period from Rosh Hashanah through Yom Kippur (the Day of Atonement). Another name is *Yamim Nora'im* (Days of Awe). The days between Rosh Hashanah and Yom Kippur, although not holidays, are a solemn time of self-searching and return. During those days, as we head toward Yom Kippur, we continue the work we did not finish on Rosh Hashanah.

HONORING AND CREATING JEWISH TRADITION

- What do you think is the most important message or lesson of Rosh Hashanah? Describe one way this teaching can help you become your best self.

  _____

  _____

  _____

  _____

- Describe a traditional Rosh Hashanah ritual or custom that you particularly enjoy, and explain why you enjoy it.

  _____

  _____

  _____

- How can you add beauty and meaning to the holiday through the tradition of _hiddur mitzvah_?

  _____

  _____

- Describe a new ritual (or an innovation to a familiar ritual) that you would like to add to the traditions of Rosh Hashanah. Explain why this addition would be appropriate and how it would add meaning or beauty to the holiday.

  _____

  _____

  _____

  _____

This tapestry by Judaic artist Lydie Egosi is called "Peace." It reminds us that on Rosh Hashanah we pray for peace for all the people of Israel and for all God's creatures.

CHAPTER 4

יוֹם כִּפּוּר

YOM KIPPUR
The Buck Stops Here

10 Tishre

Our God and God of our ancestors, forgive us, pardon us, grant us atonement.

—from the Yom Kippur prayers

On the High Holidays, the Torah scrolls are dressed in white—a symbol of purity and renewal—reminding us that the New Year provides us with the opportunity for a fresh start.

The problem is as old as humankind. When asked by God whether he had eaten from the forbidden fruit, Adam replied, "The woman *You* gave me, to be with me, *she* gave me of the tree and I did eat," accusing both God and woman in a single breath.

And when God asked Eve what had happened, she, too, tried to avoid responsibility for her actions, saying, "The *snake* led me on, and I did eat."

Too often when we yield to temptation or pressure, we argue that we should not be held accountable. But Adam and Eve *were* responsible for their actions, and so are we for ours.

Yom Kippur is a time when we are reminded that *who* we are is shaped by *what* we do. And so, acknowledging our wrongs is the first step in repairing and strengthening our character, in defining the person we *want* to be and in molding the person we *choose* to be.

Still, it is often hard to say "I am sorry." Even when our mouths speak the words, our hands may fidget or our eyes look toward the floor. The act of apologizing might not be so bad if only we didn't have to be there when we did it!

Hard as it may be to do, saying "I'm sorry" creates opportunities to repair friendships; build stronger, more thoughtful relationships; and develop our self-awareness and self-esteem. And the Jewish calendar sets aside one day a year—in fact, the holiest day of the year—as a time to focus on saying "I am sorry."

Repentance

Judaism teaches that when we hurt one person, three parties are injured: the one we offend, God, and ourselves. We must ask forgiveness from all three, but in a specific order. We must start with the one we offended, then ask for God's forgiveness; only then can we seek forgiveness from ourselves.

Certainly we don't have to wait for Yom Kippur to apologize to those we have hurt. When an appropriate occasion presents itself, we ought to take it. But sometimes we can't find, or make, the right time. So the Jewish calendar creates time for us during the month of Elul and the Ten Days of Repentance.

Of course, apologies aren't magic, nor are they all that go into making amends. They do not compensate for what was lost, nor do they magically fix things. But they can soothe an aching heart and begin to repair a damaged relationship. Our tradition teaches that after we make reasonable attempts to offer an apology, God will be moved to forgive us even if the one we have offended does not extend forgiveness.

TAKING ACTION: TESHUVAH

The Jewish community comes together on Yom Kippur to ask for God's forgiveness. But individually, we can observe the mitzvah of making *teshuvah* on any day of the year.

Write a prayer that can help you find the courage to apologize to those you have hurt.

_____

_____

Write a prayer that can help you find the compassion to forgive those who have hurt you.

_____

_____

_____

Write a prayer that can help you find the compassion to forgive yourself.

_____

_____

_____

Traveling the road to teshuvah *may not blister our feet but, at times, it can bruise our egos. When it does, how can you gain the courage to continue the journey? Might you pray? talk to a friend? listen to calming music?*

Preparing at Home

In the late afternoon, an hour or two before the holiday, families gather to eat the *se'udah mafseket,* the last meal before the fast. We do not say Kiddush, for this meal takes place before the holiday begins. In fact, we do nothing at all special at this meal, except perhaps to enjoy each bite a bit more than usual and to eat just a touch more than usual, hoping the additional food will help get us through the coming day. Yet that meal, perhaps more than any other, marks the line between our old and our renewed selves. For we are about to set off on a journey of 25 hours of reflection and imagination, and we are unlikely to leave Yom Kippur exactly as we were when the holiday began.

We fast on Yom Kippur to set aside earthly distractions, not to put our health at risk. Therefore, some people should *not* fast: the frail, those on certain medications, nursing mothers, children under the age of bar or bat mitzvah, and diabetics.

If you cannot fast, you can still share in the spirit of the day by setting boundaries on what you eat. Try avoiding favorite foods, comfort foods, sweet foods, and rich foods; you can eat far less than usual or just enough to meet your medical needs.

A *Tradition* of iNNoVāTion

Just before we go to synagogue, those who have close loved ones who have died—a father, mother, sister, brother, son, or daughter—may light a *yahrtzeit* (memorial) candle, which is designed to burn throughout the day. Although white *yahrtzeit* candles are the most commonly used, any candle that can safely remain lit into the next evening, can be used. For example, scented, colored candles, which recall the smells of the incense burned in the ancient Holy Temple, may strengthen the soul for the rigorous day ahead.

Placing yahrtzeit *candles in special, decorated ceramic holders adds to* hiddur mitzvah, *the beautification of lighting the candles.*

At the Synagogue

A bit before sundown, while the day is still light, Yom Kippur services begin. The ark is opened and all the Torah scrolls are taken out. They stand before us as escorts and witnesses, and perhaps also as protectors, as we approach God on this most holy of days. They support us and strengthen us in what we are about to do. And what we are about to do is to say two astonishing prayers.

Back to the Sources

The Torah reading on Yom Kippur includes these verses from Leviticus 16:

וְכָל־מְלָאכָה לֹא תַעֲשׂוּ הָאֶזְרָח וְהַגֵּר הַגָּר בְּתוֹכְכֶם׃ כִּי־בַיּוֹם הַזֶּה יְכַפֵּר עֲלֵיכֶם לְטַהֵר אֶתְכֶם מִכֹּל חַטֹּאתֵיכֶם לִפְנֵי יְיָ תִּטְהָרוּ׃ שַׁבַּת שַׁבָּתוֹן הִיא לָכֶם...

. . . you shall not work, neither the citizen nor the stranger who lives among you.
For on this day, atonement shall be made for you to cleanse yourself of all your sins;
you shall be clean before Adonai. It shall be a sabbath of complete rest for you. . . .

(Leviticus 16:29–31)

The first declaration says, "By the authority of the heavenly court and by the authority of the earthly court, with the consent of the One who is everywhere and with the consent of this congregation, we declare it permissible to pray with those who have done wrong."

The images of a court and a judge, so prominent in the Rosh Hashanah prayers, take center stage here. But the question is, Who are *we*, the congregation? What role do we play in this declaration? Are we the ones who are being asked to grant sinners permission to pray alongside us? Or are we those very sinners? Or are we the heavenly representatives of God's court who join these earthly proceedings? The answer is that we are all three.

Mistakes, even sins, are part of our humanity. They do not remove us from the presence of God, or from the presence of the community of Israel, or from our place among our family and friends. Rather, it is how we respond to our errors, how we correct and learn from our mistakes, that reveals who we are and who we can become.

The second astonishing declaration is the famous prayer called Kol Nidre, meaning "all vows." Recited three times by the cantor in traditional congregations, with each repetition louder than before, this declaration states that all personal vows made between ourselves and God from now until this time next year will be cancelled, will be null and void. (In the Ashkenazic—or eastern European—tradition, the declaration refers to vows made between this year and next year. In the Sephardic tradition, it refers to vows made between last year and this year.)

Why say such a prayer at the beginning of Yom Kippur? Why, at the time when we gather to promise ourselves and God that we will do better and try harder, do we recite a prayer that invalidates those promises?

One popular explanation is historical: During one period in our history, Kol Nidre offered a lifeline to desperate Jews. In Spain in the 15th century, Jews were given the following three choices: convert to Christianity, leave the country, or be killed. It was a painful if not impossible choice. Some chose death. Thousands ran away. Many went through the motions of conversion, offering their words but not their spirits. In fact, those *conversos*—called Marranos, meaning "pigs," by the Spanish, and *anusim,* meaning "those who were threatened and forced," by the Jews—secretly remained Jews. When "converting" to Christianity, they had to take an oath in the presence of a Christian court, declaring that they had turned their back on Judaism. For those Jews, the Kol Nidre prayer was a way to make their vows to Christianity empty and meaningless before God.

Yom Kippur doesn't provide a one-day cleaning service for our souls. The process of teshuvah *begins in the month of Elul, continues into Tishre and the High Holidays, and requires that we try to be our best selves throughout the year.*

Whether we pray in Hebrew or in English, we must reflect on the meaning the words of the maḥzor hold for us.

Another popular explanation for Kol Nidre is that we need to protect ourselves from our tendency to promise more than we can deliver. How many times have we promised to call? to help? to clean up? to be on time? to be more thoughtful and less impatient? How many times have we failed to follow through? If that happens in our everyday lives, how much more could it happen on Yom Kippur, when we especially seek to please God, our families, and ourselves?

But even though the Kol Nidre prayer cancels vows, the cancellation is not absolute. First, only promises made to God are cancelled—promises made to other people remain in effect and must be kept. Second, if we are able to keep the voided promises, we should. Kol Nidre forgives rather than forbids. Thus, we are still left with duties and with choices.

When Kol Nidre is over, the Torah scrolls are returned to the ark. The sky has already darkened. We are warmed up, wound up, ready. Now the real work of the day begins. We pray that we can be open to that quiet voice within, honest with ourselves and God, forgiven for our past mistakes, cautious of new ones. We pray that we can become the individuals we want to be and are capable of being.

We continue in that way for the next 25 hours, accompanied by hundreds of pages of prayers, our families and our congregation, a willing heart, and a compassionate God.

What Do You Think?

On Yom Kippur it is a tradition to dress in white. It is also a custom to avoid wearing leather shoes. This reminds us that just as we look to God to be merciful, so we too must be merciful, for example by showing concern for animals.

Do you think that dressing in white and wearing nonleather shoes on Yom Kippur can deepen our experience of the holiday and our compassion? Can it create a feeling of closeness and solidarity with other Jews? Why or why not?

_____

_____

_____

_____

In the Shelter of One Another

On Yom Kippur, Jews do not approach God alone. In our prayers, we speak in the plural: "We are Your people. . . . We are Your flock." Our tradition may teach that God judges us one by one, but it also teaches us to approach God as a group. Why would this be?

Jews are responsible for one another. We do not abandon one another in times of need. And on Yom Kippur, we stick together as a people, giving support and encouragement; and sharing the guilt, as well as the blessing.

The rabbis taught: When the pieces of parchment that make up a Torah scroll are sewn together they become holy, and it is

A JIGSAW PUZZLE

Rabbi Lawrence Kushner teaches that each of us is born with the pieces of a jigsaw puzzle we are to assemble throughout our lives. Some pieces are missing, however, and some belong to other people. It is through our interactions with others—in formal as well as in chance meetings—that the pieces get redistributed and each person's puzzle takes shape. We need one another to complete who we are.

How do you help your friends become complete?

_____

_____

How do your friends help complete you?

_____

_____

Describe how someone you have never met has helped to complete you. For example, you may have been influenced by a person whom you read about in the newspaper, an author whose books you enjoy, an athlete whom you admire, or a biblical or historical figure.

_____

_____

_____

_____

_____

_____

_____

What are the qualities you look for in a friend? What qualities do you offer as a friend?

forbidden to erase even one letter. But when the Torah scroll is still in segments, it is permissible to make an erasure. That concept represents the souls of the Jewish people—when united, none may blot them out.

In this spirit, when we recite the Ashamnu, an alphabetic list of our sins, we use the plural: *Ashamnu, we* are guilty; *bagadnu, we* betrayed; *gazalnu,* we stole; *we* spoke ill of others; *we* were stubborn; *we* gave bad advice; *we* acted badly and caused others to act badly.

Do the words imply that each of us is guilty of the entire list? Of course not. Rather, it indicates that although each of us may have committed only one or two of these acts, we are nonetheless capable of committing all of them. We cover for one another.

Yet another alphabetic prayer of confession is the Al Ḥet, which stretches on for pages. As we confess sin after sin, we wonder how we can ever rise above our past weaknesses, or ever again resist their temptation, for there are so many of them and we are so small. Then, like a ladder reaching down to us from above, the prayer calls on us to climb, hope, and remember: Repentance, prayer, and tzedakah can strengthen our spirit and pave the road to forgiveness.

ONE PEOPLE, MANY CUSTOMS:
Kneeling

The highlight of Yom Kippur in the time of the Holy Temple was a special service at which the High Priest officiated and humbly kneeled before God. Today, we read descriptions of this service on Yom Kippur. During the recitation, in many synagogues, the cantor and rabbi kneel, as do some congregants.

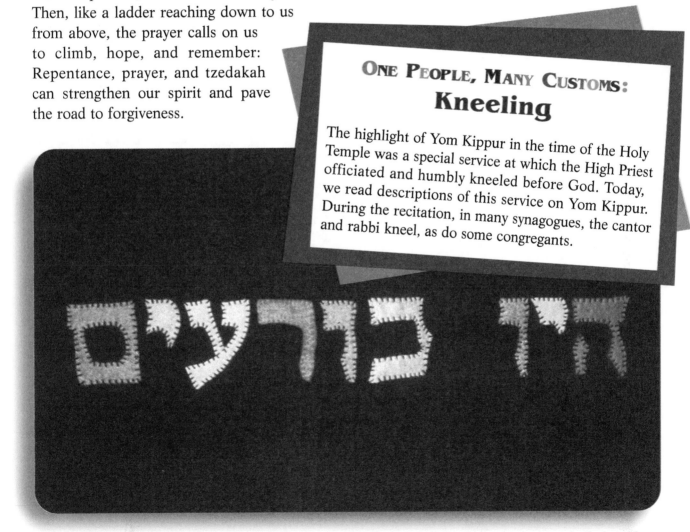

This kneeler, made by Judaic artist Naomi Hordes, is placed on the floor to protect one's clothes when kneeling in prayer. The Hebrew text says, "They (the priests) would kneel."

Jonah

One of the highlights of the day is the afternoon *haftarah,* the chanting of the Book of Jonah. Jonah was a prophet called on by God to tell the people of Nineveh that they would be destroyed if they did not stop their wicked behavior. Jonah tried to avoid his duty by boarding a ship he hoped would carry him away from God's watchful eyes. But the ship hit turbulent waters, and Jonah, believing that it was God's doing and that he was endangering the lives of the crew, had himself tossed overboard, whereupon he was swallowed by a giant fish. After three days and nights, the fish spit Jonah out onto dry land.

Jonah understood what had happened and why, so he went to warn the people of Nineveh. When they heard his prophecy, they repented and changed their ways, and God spared them. But Jonah was angry.

Becoming the Hands of God

The story of Jonah is a reminder that each of us can be the "hands of God"—a reminder that God is present in the world.

Describe a circumstance in which you acted as God's hands in the past year.

_____

_____

_____

_____

_____

Describe two ways in which you plan to act as God's hands in the new year.

_____

_____

_____

_____

_____

Jonah speaking to the people of Nineveh

Imagine that you are a member of your synagogue's social justice committee. Write a proposal for an activity in which members can act as God's hands. For example, you might propose that your synagogue organize a food, clothing, or blood drive, or that a demonstation be held in support of an oppressed minority group.

What I think should be done:

_____

_____

_____

Why the project is important to the people I want to help:

_____

_____

How it reinforces a lesson of Yom Kippur and can strengthen our congregation:

_____

_____

_____

_____

Jews have puzzled over Jonah's behavior for thousands of years. Why did Jonah try to run away from God, who, our tradition teaches, is everywhere and knows everything? Why did Jonah get angry after he helped save the lives of 120,000 people? And why do we read that book on Yom Kippur?

The Book of Jonah teaches us many lessons: that the purpose of Yom Kippur is not to punish us but rather to help us find the good inside ourselves; that we are responsible for one another; that we become the hands of God through the mitzvot we do, such as feeding the hungry; and that we cannot hide from ourselves or from God.

Many synagogues begin social justice projects by inviting the community to study Torah together. In what ways do you think such study can add meaning to our actions?

Ne'ilah, the Closing of the Gates

At the very end of the day, when the sun has slipped below the horizon, after reciting the prayers on hundreds of pages, after saying Ashamnu and Al Het eight times, we add one more service: Ne'ilah, a confession pleading with God to be kind and compassionate.

But just in case our voices have become weak or our tears have dried up, we blow the shofar: *tekiah gedolah,* the longest, greatest shofar sound of all. One last cry of sorrow, one last cry of hope, one last chance to stir God's mercy. A powerful sound, it seems to gain in strength the longer it is held. And for a moment, through the shofar, our voices become one.

With that, court is adjourned until the next year. Everyone wishes friends and loved ones a healthy, happy New Year. Next year in Jerusalem! לְשָׁנָה הַבָּאָה בִּירוּשָׁלָיִם! The praying is done, the confessions complete: We end as we started, in God's hands, only more hopeful and perhaps more trusting.

HONORING AND CREATING JEWISH TRADITION

- What do you think is the most important message or lesson of Yom Kippur? How can this teaching help you become a better son or daughter? a better friend?

  _____

  _____

  _____

  _____

- Describe a traditional Yom Kippur ritual or custom that is particularly important to you, and explain why it is important.

  _____

  _____

  _____

- How can you add beauty and meaning to the holiday through the tradition of _hiddur mitzvah_?

  _____

  _____

- Describe a new ritual (or an innovation to a familiar ritual) that you would like to add to the traditions of Yom Kippur. Explain why this addition would be appropriate and how it would add meaning or beauty to the holiday.

  _____

  _____

  _____

  _____

  _____

This tapestry by Lydie Egosi is called "Offerings to God." In what way can praying be considered an offering to God? What other actions might also be considered offerings to God? Why?

CHAPTER 5

סֻכּוֹת

SUKKOT
The Journey and the Harvest

15–21 Tishre

Be seated, be seated, exalted guests. Be seated, be seated, holy guests. Sit in the shade of the Holy One, blessed be the One.

—from the greeting welcoming ancestral guests into the sukkah

Decorating a sukkah is lots of fun. You can make ornaments out of paper or clay and hang colorful fruits and vegetables.

When our ancestors left Egypt on their journey to freedom, they took with them enough food and water for only a few days. When their provisions ran out, so did their trust in God. And so did their desire for freedom. They ranted against Moses and Aaron, and wailed, "If only we had died by the hand of God in the Land of Egypt . . . for you have brought us out into this wilderness to starve this entire community to death!" (Exodus 16:3).

But God heard the Israelites' cries and had compassion. Tradition teaches that, to ease their thirst, God created a well of fresh water—Miriam's well, it would be called—that followed them wherever they went. To ease their hunger, God created manna, a frosty-white, doughlike food that appeared with the morning dew and took on the flavor of anything the Israelites wanted.

And yet, no matter how God tried, no matter how God threatened or promised, these former slaves would not accept the risks and responsibilities of a free people.

The Torah tells us that when the Israelites were in the wilderness, Moses went up Mount Sinai and stayed there for 40 days to receive the Law from God. In his absence, the Israelites' faith weakened. When he returned with the tablets of the Ten Commandments and saw the Israelites worshipping a Golden Calf—an idol—Moses broke the tablets.

So God kept the Israelites in the wilderness for 40 years, enough time for the younger generation, adventurous and responsible, to become leaders. And when, at last, that generation was ready, God led them into the Promised Land, the Land of Israel.

The Holiday of Journeys

Sukkot commemorates our people's journey from oppression in Egypt, through the Sinai wilderness where we were given the Torah, and on to the Promised Land. It is the holiday that best symbolizes our own experience as we journey through life: sometimes moving, sometimes stuck, but heading—we hope—in the right direction and learning to improve ourselves along the way.

The word *sukkot* means "shelters," a comforting image in contrast to the unfamiliarity and insecurity that often accompany travel. It refers to the temporary booths we build and eat in on this holiday. The sacred story of Sukkot reminds us of the Israelites' travels in the desert over a period of 40 years and of how they were protected and fed by God. The agricultural story reminds us of the time when our ancestors were farmers in the Land of Israel. To ease their work during the fall harvest, and to avoid the need to trek the long way home every night, they would build booths to live in, far out in the fields.

Sukkot reminds us that, ultimately, our security is found not within the walls of our home but in the presence of God and one another. This holiday helps us understand that sometimes the concrete and steel walls we build to protect us serve instead to divide us, cut us off, lock us in. In contrast, the flimsy walls of our sukkot make us more available to receive one another's kindness and support, to hear when others call out in need, to poke our heads in to see whether anybody is up for a chat and a snack. Sukkot reminds us that freedom is enjoyed best not when we are hidden away behind locked doors but rather when we are able to open our homes and our hearts to one another.

How Our Ancestors Celebrated

In the time of the Holy Temple, Sukkot was the most festive of the pilgrimage holidays, celebrated with music and dancing, bonfires, and jugglers and many other entertainers. It was a time of lavish parades around the Temple, with Jews, holding lulav and etrog in hand, singing prayers asking God to protect and save them.

The ancient rabbis believed that on Sukkot, God determines how much rain will fall during the coming year. In the time of the

The Pilgrimage Holidays

Sukkot is one of the three pilgrimage holidays—the other two being Passover and Shavuot. Each of the holidays has two stories that are told about it, one historical and the other agricultural. Sukkot reminds us of the 40 years that the Jews wandered in the desert and marks the end of the summer harvest. Passover celebrates the Exodus and the beginning of the spring harvest. Shavuot celebrates the giving of the Torah on Mount Sinai and the end of the barley harvest.

The pilgrimage holidays are called *regalim*, from the Hebrew word for "foot" or "leg" (*regel*), for Jews were to make their way (on foot) to Jerusalem on each of these holidays.

On Sukkot we are reminded that often a thoughtful or loving gesture is all we need to feel secure.

Temple, water ceremonies with torches and song were held on Sukkot. They would involve the whole city: children from the priestly class; men and women; old and young; and "men of deeds," who were given the honor of leading the way. The rabbis said that you have not seen real celebration if you have never seen *Simḥat Beit Hasho'evah,* the Sukkot celebration in the Temple.

How We Celebrate

The sukkah is the central symbol of this holiday of journeys. It is a temporary structure in which we are to live for one week. Most people today decorate it with pictures and hangings, place a table and chairs in it, invite guests and eat there. Some Jews even sleep in the sukkah.

The structure of the sukkah, as determined by the rabbis of the Talmud, must follow certain rules. It can't be higher than 30 feet, for if it were it would look permanent. It must have at least three walls, or else it will look too flimsy. The roof, called *sechach,* must be made of cut branches or leaves to remind us of the harvest. The covering can't be too thin or too full. In the daytime the roof must offer more shade than sun, while at night, the stars should be seen through the branches and leaves.

But there is more to Sukkot than eating or sleeping in a sukkah.

ONE PEOPLE, MANY CUSTOMS:
Special Guests

Along with friends and relatives, we invite *ushpizin*, seven patriarchal leaders of old—Abraham, Isaac, Jacob, Joseph, Moses, Aaron, and David—to join us for a meal in the sukkah.

Today, some people also invite seven matriarchal leaders, or *ushpizot*, often Sarah, Rebecca, Rachel, Leah, Miriam, Deborah, and Ruth. Many families also invite favorite relatives who are no longer alive and who are sorely missed. Some families create an *ushpizin* or *ushpizot* mural that includes the names, sayings, and remembrances of loved ones whom they want to invite. Dinners become times of recollecting. We can tell the stories of the lives of our loved ones, repeat their favorite sayings, share their jokes, recite their achievements.

Name two people whom you would like to invite as *ushpizin* or *ushpizot* and explain why.

_____

_____

_____

_____

_____

_____

This ushpizot *mural was created by artist Ellen Alt. It honors seven matriarchal leaders and beautifies the sukkah.*

Just as the sukkah provided our ancestors with shelter during the journey from enslavement to freedom in their own land, so today the sukkah can provide a place of shelter as we make our own emotional and spiritual journeys. During the Ten Days of Awe we reviewed the past year, set new goals, and became determined to reach higher in the new year, to become the best people we can be.

Gathering our friends and family around us, standing outside the sukkah, we now can express our commitment to change and our gratitude for the love and support of all those who are present. One by one, our friends can enter the sukkah, demonstrating that we do not have to make this crossing alone. When we are ready, we step across the threshold, entering a new space in which we can grow.

Sukkot is also a time of harvest and thanksgiving, when we show our gratitude to God for sustaining us on our journey through life. In the words of Torah, we are instructed to "take the product of goodly trees [etrog], branches of palm trees [lulav], boughs of leafy trees [hadasim] and willows of the brook [aravot], and . . . rejoice before Adonai, your God, seven days" (Leviticus 23:40).

Therefore, every day during Sukkot, except on Shabbat, we take four symbols *(arba'ah minim)* of the earth's bounty—the lulav (a palm branch) adorned with myrtle and willow, and an etrog (a citron)—and shake them in six directions.

We hold the lulav, myrtle, and willow in the right hand, much as we would hold a banner or a flag. And we hold the etrog—which looks like a large, bumpy lemon and smells even more fragrant—in

This woodblock print shows Polish Jews celebrating Sukkot over 100 years ago. At the bottom, in Hebrew, is a quote from Leviticus 23:42: "You shall live in sukkot seven days."

the left. When we first pick up the lulav and the etrog, we bring the two together (with the stem, or *pitam,* of the etrog pointing downward) and recite the blessing.

Then we turn the etrog over so that the *pitam* is facing up, and—still holding our hands together—we shake the lulav and the etrog in front, to the right, in back, to the left, up and down. We do this as if to say, "Do you see these, World? They represent the goodness that God has given us, and we are very grateful."

Back to the Sources

We recite the following blessing before shaking the lulav and etrog:

בָּרוּךְ אַתָּה, יְיָ אֱלֹהֵינוּ, מֶלֶךְ הָעוֹלָם, אֲשֶׁר קִדְּשָׁנוּ בְּמִצְוֹתָיו וְצִוָּנוּ עַל נְטִילַת לוּלָב.

Blessed are You, Adonai our God, Sovereign of the universe, who has sanctified us through Your mitzvot and commands us to take the lulav.

What Do You Think?

Rabbi Harold Schulweis shares this teaching of his grandfather: Jewish law states that if guests are invited to the sukkah on the first night and rain begins to fall, one should wait until midnight to eat in the sukkah. Perhaps the rain will stop by that time. But if the guests are poor, one should not wait for the rain to stop. Being poor, they may not have eaten all day. Let them eat with you in the dining room and forgo the mitzvah of dwelling in the sukkah.

What important lesson does this story teach?

_____

_____

_____

_____

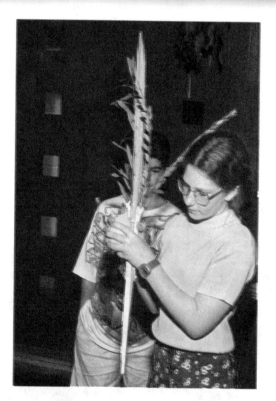

When reciting the blessing over the lulav and etrog, it is traditional to stand.

TAKING ACTION: FEEDING THE HUNGRY

On Sukkot, we remember that God protected the Israelites and provided manna for them to eat as they wandered through the Sinai wilderness. We turn the memory into mitzvot when we help the homeless find shelter and fulfill the mitzvah of feeding the hungry, *ma'achil re'evim*.

Many communities have organizations that collect food from restaurants, caterers, and hotels and bring it to soup kitchens and other centers for the hungry. You can use the holiday of Sukkot as a time to encourage your synagogue to sign a pledge to contribute to such an organization whenever the synagogue holds an event at which food is served.

How else can you work with others to help bring the earth's bounty to people who are hungry?

_____

_____

_____

_____

How can your pleasure in decorating and eating in a sukkah remind you to share the goodness of your "harvest" with others?

Light Bulbs: Sharing Your Bright Ideas

Imagine that you are a member of a synagogue committee whose goal it is to bring the members of your congregation together during Sukkot to enjoy the holiday and to help those in need. What might you want to do? Hold a sukkah decorating party or a potluck dinner at which people contribute canned foods for those in need? Hold a sleepover at your synagogue, inviting everyone to also work in a local shelter on one night of the holiday? How about baking and decorating a gingerbread sukkah that you auction off as a fund-raiser to help feed the poor?

Describe the activity you have in mind and outline a plan to organize and promote it.

_____

_____

_____

_____

_____

_____

_____

_____

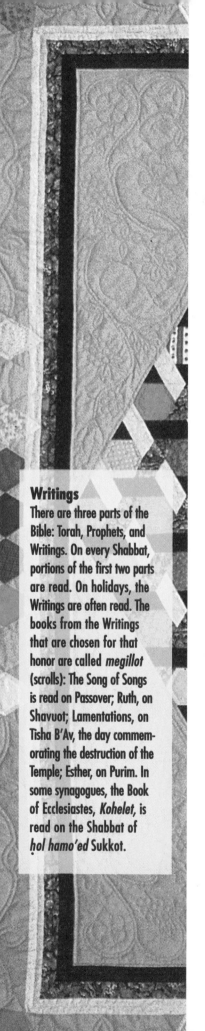

Reform and Reconstructionist Jews and the Jews of Israel celebrate Sukkot for eight days, observing the first day and last day as full holidays. Conservative and Orthodox Jews of the Diaspora (Jews living outside of Israel) celebrate Sukkot for nine days, observing the first two days and the last two days (a remnant of the difficulty of proclaiming the New Moon for Jews beyond the reach of the Rosh Ḥodesh signal—see page 15). The whole day (or two) is devoted to celebration. The pilgrimage holidays are similar to Shabbat in their observance: no work, no business, no school, no shopping, no building.

The remaining five (or six) days are the intermediate days, *ḥol hamo'ed.* We recite the special holiday prayers, shake the lulav and etrog every morning, and eat our meals in the sukkah. But we go to work or school, shop, watch movies—in other words, do anything we would do on a normal day unless, of course, it is also Shabbat.

Inviting friends for a meal in your own or your synagogue's sukkah can help make the holiday more joyous and meaningful, not to mention more fun.

The period of the *Yamim Nora'im,* the High Holidays, does not completely end until the seventh day of Sukkot, the day called Hoshana Rabba. Hoshana means "please save us" and refers to the lengthy version of the prayer we say during the morning services throughout Sukkot. On the other days of the holiday, we recite the prayer, called Hoshanot, while moving around the sanctuary once. On Hoshana Rabba, we recite that prayer while making seven circuits. It is on that day, the rabbis tell us, that the Book of Judgment is finally sealed. On that day, we take the willow branches from our lulav and beat them on the ground, a final act of regret for all that we have done wrong.

HONORING AND CREATING JEWISH TRADITION

- What do you think is the most important message or lesson of Sukkot? Describe one way this teaching can help you become your best self.

  _____

  _____

  _____

  _____

- Describe a traditional Sukkot ritual or custom that you particularly enjoy, and explain why you enjoy it.

  _____

  _____

  _____

- How can you add beauty and meaning to the holiday through the tradition of _hiddur mitzvah_, whether or not you have a sukkah at home?

  _____

  _____

- Describe a new ritual (or an innovation to a familiar ritual) that you would like to add to the traditions of Sukkot. Explain why this addition would be appropriate and how it would add meaning or beauty to the holiday.

  _____

  _____

  _____

  _____

  _____

This quilt by artist Sheila Groman is called "Mishkan Star."
After the Israelites received the Torah, they built and then carried
the Mishkan—_the Tabernacle—through the Sinai wilderness. It_
symbolized that God's presence was always with them.

CHAPTER 6

שִׂמְחַת תּוֹרָה

SIMḤAT TORAH
Scrolling Through the Year

22/23 Tishre

Turn [the Torah] again and again, for everything is in it; contemplate it, grow gray and old over it, and swerve not from it for there is no greater good.

—Ben Bag Bag, Mishnah, Avot 5:22

Torah scrolls are carried with great care and love.

W hat is your favorite song? Have you ever played it over and over on a CD player, and maybe in your mind? Have you ever read a favorite book several times or seen the same movie so often that you practically knew all the lines by heart? What made you want to repeat the experience again and again? Did you enjoy sharing your experience with others? Why?

Similarly, why, each Shabbat, do Jews around the world, read and study the week's Torah portion—called the *parashah* or *sidrah*—in synagogue? Why do you think that even though it takes one full year to complete the cycle of 54 portions, as soon as we have finished, we roll the Torah scroll back to the beginning and start over again?

It is because of our great love of Torah, and because Torah keeps the Jewish people strong and alive. The importance of Torah can be demonstrated by the legend of Rabbi Akiva, who lived in the Land of Israel when the Romans ruled. Although the Romans forbade the study of Torah, Rabbi Akiva continued his studies. When asked why he was willing to risk his life for the sake of studying Torah, Rabbi Akiva explained, "Just as fish need water to live, so the Jewish people need Torah. Though it may be dangerous to continue studying, it would be far more dangerous to stop." And with that, the rabbi smiled and returned to his studies.

Simḥat Torah means "Rejoicing of the Torah" and is celebrated on the last day of Sukkot. It is one of the most joyous holidays of the Jewish year: After completing the year's reading of the Torah, we are happy to begin the cycle once again.

The Last Two Days of Sukkot

The last day (or two days) of Sukkot are really additional holidays: Shemini Atzeret and Simḥat Torah. In Israel and in many Reconstructionist and Reform congregations in the Diaspora, Shemini Atzeret and Simḥat Torah are celebrated together on the eighth day. For others, Shemini Atzeret is the eighth day of the holiday, and Simḥat Torah is the ninth.

Sukkot marks the end of the growing season in Israel and the beginning of the rainy, wintry season. The earth lies dormant, inactive, until the first stirrings of spring. In ancient Israel, Shemini Atzeret was the closing of the Sukkot festival.

After the Temple was destroyed, Shemini Atzeret became a holiday without a ritual. We are not asked to eat and sleep in the sukkah on Shemini Atzeret, nor do we shake the lulav and etrog. Shemini Atzeret became a holiday in search of a cause. So its character was taken over by Simḥat Torah. Simḥat Torah, after all, is really the second day of Shemini Atzeret.

The beauty of this Holy Ark and the ornaments on the Torah scrolls reflect our traditions of love of Torah and hiddur mitzvah.

What Do You Think?

Two Talmudic sages, Rabbi Tarfon and Rabbi Akiva, struggled to determine which is more important—studying Torah or living according to its laws. Rabbi Tarfon was convinced that it is more important to follow the laws of Torah. Rabbi Akiva argued that the only way to know what the laws are is to study Torah.

In the end, the sages determined that the study of Torah is greater than all the other mitzvot because it leads to them all.

Do you agree with the sages? Why or why not?

_____

_____

_____

_____

_____

_____

_____

A TREE OF LIFE

Because the Torah gives life and strength to the Jewish people, it often is called *Etz Ḥayyim,* a Tree of Life. In the space below, write a poem or draw a picture that expresses your vision of the Torah as a Tree of Life.

TAKING ACTION: ACTS OF LOVINGKINDNESS

When we study Torah, we learn how to do our part to improve the world through acts of lovingkindness—*gemilut ḥasadim*—such as helping our parents when they are tired or feeling ill, welcoming a new classmate, and comforting or feeding a pet. Acts of *gemilut ḥasadim* strengthen the caring relationships among people, and between people and God's other creatures.

What acts of lovingkindness have you performed this week?

_____

_____

How can studying Torah remind you to perform such acts all year round?

_____

_____

Not only does Judaism forbid us to harm others, for example, by placing "a stumbling block before the blind" (Leviticus 19:14), but it also instructs us to perform acts of lovingkindness, such as offering to help a blind person cross the street.

Back to the Sources

The Torah tells us that immediately after Sukkot

בַּיּוֹם הַשְּׁמִינִי עֲצֶרֶת תִּהְיֶה לָכֶם כָּל־מְלֶאכֶת עֲבֹדָה
לֹא תַעֲשׂוּ:

On the eighth day, you shall hold a solemn assembly [atzeret]; you shall not work at your occupations. (Numbers 29:35)

That is all we know about Shemini Atzeret from the Torah. Some people think it was a formal way to bring an end to Sukkot, the last harvest celebration of the agricultural year.

How We Celebrate

On Simḥat Torah, we read the Torah at night—something that is not done in Conservative and Orthodox congregations at any other time of the year. In the middle of the evening service, the Torah scrolls are taken out of the ark, often to the accompaniment of singing and dancing. Usually we remove only the scroll that we will read from on that day. But on Simḥat Torah we take *all* the scrolls from the ark.

On other days of the year, we make only one ceremonial *hakafah*, or circuit, around the synagogue with the Torah. On Simḥat Torah, we make seven *hakafot* (the plural of *hakafah*). On other days of the year, the *hakafah* is conducted simply, generally to the accompaniment of a single song, and lasts only a few minutes. On Simḥat Torah, the *hakafot* are more like parades, spirited processions, accompanied by many joyous songs. We clear away the seats and dance with energy and spirit. On other days, only a few people walk around the sanctuary escorting the Torah, but on Simḥat Torah, everyone joins in. On other days, only one person holds the Torah when it is taken out of the ark. On Simḥat Torah, the Torah scrolls are held by every Jew who desires.

ONE PEOPLE, MANY CUSTOMS:
Torah Mantle or Case

One way we show our love and respect for the Torah is by using beautiful coverings and ornaments to dress the Torah scroll. A mantle—or coat—covers the scroll in Ashkenazic synagogues. In Sephardic synagogues, the scroll is often kept in a case made of wood decorated with leather or metal. The case opens into two sections.

But, sooner or later the singing and dancing stops. We set the Torah scrolls back in the ark, except the one from which we will read. We open to the last *parashah* of Deuteronomy, the last book of the Five Books of Moses. Those verses record the farewell blessing Moses made over the children of Israel on the banks of the Jordan River, just before he died. We read all but the last lines, which tell of Moses' death. We save those for the morning; they are too sad to be read on this night. Then the Torah is put away, and we finish the evening service.

*A Sephardic case
for a Torah scroll*

An increasingly popular tradition is the unrolling of the entire Torah scroll on Simḥat Torah. All are invited to participate in the ritual. Column upon column, white space and black ink, the letters of the Torah reflect the majesty and beauty of the Torah, decorated as they are with crowns.

In the morning, we again take out all the Torah scrolls and make seven *hakafot* around the synagogue. After the *hakafot,* the Torah reading begins again. We read the same verses that we read the night before, repeating them again and again so that everyone who wants one can be honored with an *aliyah.* After all the adults (that is, anyone over the age of bat or bar mitzvah) who wish to have had an *aliyah,* the children are called up together to the *bimah,* the platform from which the Torah is read. They gather under a tallit for an *aliyah* called *kol hana'arim* (all the children). An adult accompanies them and says the blessings for them.

On Simḥat Torah many synagogues welcome new students to the tradition of Jewish learning by holding a ceremony called a "consecration." The children are called up to the bimah. *They may be taught the first line of the Sh'ma, gathered under a tallit, blessed with the good wishes of the congregation, and given a certificate or gift.*

Imagine that you are the chairperson of your synagogue's religious school committee and you have been asked to speak at the consecration ceremony on Simḥat Torah. Write a brief speech to help children who are between the ages of six and eight understand the Jewish people's love of Torah and the importance of studying Torah.

_____

_____

_____

_____

_____

_____

_____

_____

_____

_____

_____

Only then, after everyone who wants an *aliyah* has had one, are the last verses of the Torah read. When a man is honored with that *aliyah* he is given the title *ḥatan Torah* (bridegroom of the Torah) and when the honor goes to a woman she is called the *kallat Torah* (bride of the Torah). Sometimes a couple receives this honor.

Why bride and bridegroom? Because these words remind us of the vision of the people of Israel and God as bride and groom, respectively, and inspire images of Mount Sinai, when God and the Israelites pledged to be true to each other. On Simḥat Torah, these titles serve as symbols of our renewed vow to God, our partner in the *Brit*.

We feel the sadness of the Israelites as they watched Moses go up the mountain, this time never to return. We imagine how alone they must have felt and how frightened, losing the only leader they had ever known. But this, too, is the message of Simḥat Torah: that Judaism is greater than any one person or any one moment, that with God and the Torah we are never really alone.

So we put aside our sadness, close the first Torah scroll, call up the *ḥatan* or *kallat B'reshit* (bridegroom or bride of Genesis), open to the first lines of Genesis in the second Torah scroll, and begin all over again.

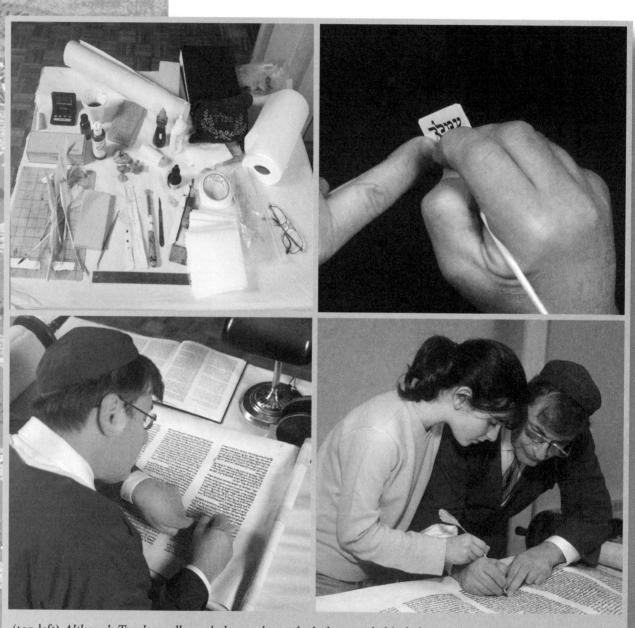

(top left) *Although Torah scrolls are holy, we do not lock them up behind glass—we use them. And because we use them, they sometimes need to be repaired. A sofer, or scribe, requires many tools to perform the sacred work of repairing a scroll.* (top right) *Each day before beginning to write or repair a Torah scroll, a sofer writes, then crosses out, the name of the Israelites' archenemy, Amalek.* (bottom left) *When words on the parchment have been badly damaged, before making the repair, the* sofer *checks the spelling in a printed copy of the Torah called a* tikkun. *You can see the* tikkun *at the top center of the photograph.* (bottom right) *A student assists the* sofer.

HONORING AND CREATING JEWISH TRADITION

- What do you think is the most important message or lesson of Simḥat Torah? Describe one way this teaching can help you become your best self.

  _____

  _____

  _____

  _____

- Describe a traditional Simḥat Torah ritual or custom that you particularly enjoy, and explain why you enjoy it.

  _____

  _____

  _____

- How can you add beauty and meaning to the holiday through the tradition of _hiddur mitzvah_?

  _____

  _____

- Describe a new ritual (or an innovation to a familiar ritual) that you would like to add to the traditions of Simḥat Torah. Explain why this addition would be appropriate and how it would add meaning or beauty to the holiday.

  _____

  _____

  _____

  _____

  _____

  _____

This handmade Torah mantle by artist Peachy Levy includes knotted stitches that symbolize words of Torah and golden beads that symbolize human acts of righteousness. What symbols might you want to put on a Torah mantle? Why?

CHAPTER 7

SHABBAT
A Palace in Time

*Even more than the Jews have kept Shabbat,
Shabbat has kept the Jews.*

—Aḥad Ha'am

Setting a beautiful Shabbat table not only enriches our observance of Shabbat, but also enhances Jewish tradition, for we are an integral part of the tradition, and what we do makes a difference.

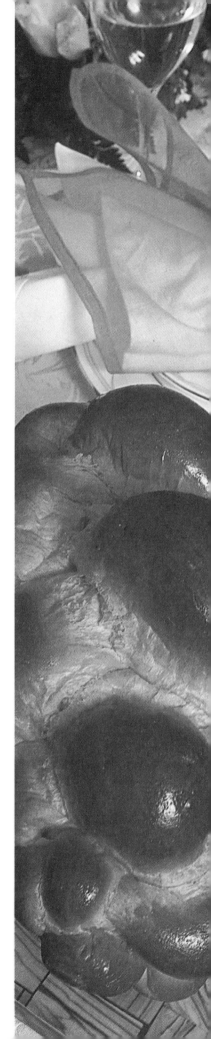

Every seventh sunset, Shabbat comes. Whether we welcome it or not, on the seventh day, Shabbat awaits us. Shabbat is different from all the other holidays. It does not mark a historical event or a seasonal harvest. Its arrival does not depend upon the phases of the moon. Our tradition teaches that Shabbat existed even before there was a Jewish people. Shabbat is truly God's holiday, a remembrance of the seventh day of Creation, the day of completion and rest.

This holy day was given as a gift to the Jewish people as our ancestors, the Israelites, stood at the foot of Mount Sinai. Ever since then Shabbat has been called an *ot,* a sign—an eternal reminder that God is *our* God, with whom we have a sacred covenant.

God's Dream for Our World

Rabbi Abraham Joshua Heschel called Shabbat "a palace in time," a holy place that arrives and opens its doors to us once a week, inviting us to enter. Six days of the week we live in our world, busying ourselves with the tasks and responsibilities of school, home, and friendships. Sometimes in this world we can feel God's touch. It may happen when we feel the love and comfort of a parent's embrace, when we hold a newborn infant in our arms, or when we pause to thank a friend or stranger for help.

Sometimes we are aware of these feelings of godliness. But it is difficult to hold onto them amid the hustle and bustle of our everyday world. In contrast, on Shabbat we are invited to enter God's dream for our world, a place of peace, abundance, and caring.

In our world, work is essential because Creation is incomplete. There is much to do and much to achieve—so many houses to build, so many mouths to feed, things to discover, people to tend to. "For six days you shall do your work," the fourth commandment tells us.

But if we never stopped working, we might become so caught up in the tasks we are doing that we would forget *why* we are doing them. We might forget that our purpose is to help complete Creation so that all God's creatures can live together in peace and harmony.

Learning the Way of Menuḥah

Every seventh day, therefore, our tradition asks us to set aside quiet time, to stop working, to follow in God's ways by resting on the seventh day.

The Hebrew word for this rest and quiet is *menuḥah,* and it refers exclusively to the rest we experience on Shabbat. Although work may be forbidden on other holidays, that rest is not called *menuḥah.*

Shabbat asks us to clear our calendars on Friday night and Saturday so we can spend time at home and in the synagogue, with our families, our friends, and our community. Shabbat asks that we take the time to be with the ones we love and enjoy the pleasures of God's Creation. It invites us to sing and play and read and eat and talk and sleep and love. Shabbat asks that we not cook or shop, that we not build anything or fix anything or sew anything or grow anything. Shabbat is a taste of God's dream for our world.

The Limits of Living "As If"
Judaism recognizes that no matter how much Shabbat is a vision of God's dreamworld, reality sometimes intrudes. People will still get sick on Shabbat and will still need others to help them on Shabbat. So great is the mitzvah of saving a life that it overrides the restrictions of Shabbat. Therefore on Shabbat, if someone is seriously ill or has been in an accident and we can help, we *must* help—even if it means breaking the laws of Shabbat. In Hebrew, this is called *pikuaḥ nefesh*, the overriding importance of saving a life.

Tzedakah
For generations, just before Shabbat, families have had the tradition of putting money for the needy in a tzedakah box. They put in pennies, nickels, dimes, or quarters. When the box is full, the family members count up the money and decide where it should be sent.

Twice a year—during the week before Rosh Hashanah and the week before Passover—it is traditional to be extra generous in the giving of tzedakah. Your preparation for those holidays might include the distribution of the money you have collected. A month before, you can research your favorite causes, then present the options for giving to your family so you can make the decision together.

Just as this road sign in Israel reminds drivers that the speed limit is 80 kilometers per hour, so on Shabbat we may need reminders to slow down. What can help you remember to change gears and observe Shabbat?

Through a Magic Doorway

When the sun goes down on the sixth day and we light the Shabbat candles, we open a doorway in time and space. We stand before the candlesticks. We circle our hands above the flames three times, gathering, collecting, bathing ourselves in their light. We cup our hands as if scooping up their glow, carrying it gently toward our eyes. We recite the blessing over the candles.

Although the blessing mentions only one candle, most households traditionally light two. Some families light one candle for each child. Other families light one candle for each member of the household.

Back to the Sources

On Friday night we recite the following blessing over the Shabbat candles:

בָּרוּךְ אַתָּה, יְיָ אֱלֹהֵינוּ, מֶלֶךְ הָעוֹלָם, אֲשֶׁר קִדְּשָׁנוּ בְּמִצְוֹתָיו וְצִוָּנוּ לְהַדְלִיק נֵר שֶׁל שַׁבָּת.

Blessed are You, Adonai our God, Sovereign of the universe, who has sanctified us through Your mitzvot and commands us to light the Shabbat candles.

Ushering in Shabbat

On Friday night—*erev Shabbat*—we greet the seventh day with a synagogue service called *kabbalat Shabbat,* the welcoming of Shabbat. Traditionally, *kabbalat Shabbat* begins at or just before sunset and lasts about an hour. However, to accommodate those who return home from work late or eat dinner with their families first, some synagogues begin *kabbalat Shabbat* later. The prayers of the service speak, and sing, of the wonders of God as Creator, of the promises that God makes to Israel, and of the wondrous gift of Shabbat. Sometimes, especially after late Friday night services, the congregation sponsors an *oneg Shabbat,* where congregants come together for refreshments and conversation.

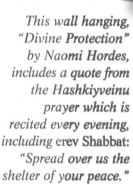

This wall hanging, "Divine Protection" by Naomi Hordes, includes a quote from the Hashkiyveinu prayer which is recited every evening, including erev Shabbat: *"Spread over us the shelter of your peace."*

Shabbat Dinner

Shabbat is the only day of Creation to receive a blessing (Genesis 2:3); in fact, it has become a day full of blessings. Dinner begins with Kiddush, the prayer that speaks of the holiness of the day.

Back to the Sources

The words of the Kiddush recall the very first Shabbat, described in Genesis:

וַיְהִי־עֶרֶב וַיְהִי־בֹקֶר יוֹם הַשִּׁשִּׁי: . . .

וַיְכֻלּוּ הַשָּׁמַיִם וְהָאָרֶץ וְכָל־צְבָאָם: וַיְכַל אֱלֹהִים

בַּיּוֹם הַשְּׁבִיעִי מְלַאכְתּוֹ אֲשֶׁר עָשָׂה וַיִּשְׁבֹּת

בַּיּוֹם הַשְּׁבִיעִי מִכָּל־מְלַאכְתּוֹ אֲשֶׁר עָשָׂה:

וַיְבָרֶךְ אֱלֹהִים אֶת־יוֹם הַשְּׁבִיעִי וַיְקַדֵּשׁ

אֹתוֹ כִּי בוֹ שָׁבַת מִכָּל־מְלַאכְתּוֹ אֲשֶׁר־בָּרָא

אֱלֹהִים לַעֲשׂוֹת:

. . . And it was evening and it was morning, the sixth day. The heavens and the earth and all they contain were complete. On the seventh day, God completed the work and rested on the seventh day from all the work. And God blessed the seventh day and made it holy, for on that day, God rested from all the work that God had intended to do. (1:31–2:3)

ONE PEOPLE, MANY CUSTOMS:
The Choreography of Kiddush

Kiddush can be made in many ways. In some homes, one adult (or one child) recites the Kiddush for everyone. In others, each person recites it, one after the other. In still others, everyone sings Kiddush together. In some homes, everyone begins the meal with a cup filled to the brim, while in others, the leader holds a broad, full cup and after Kiddush pours a bit from that cup into the others' cups. In yet other homes, there is one Kiddush cup from which everyone drinks, signifying that we all share a common tradition.

Different families have different customs. For example, some families stand when reciting the blessing over wine; others sit. Jewish tradition teaches that guests should follow the customs of the place they are visiting —the minhag hamakom.

It is customary for parents to bless their children at the dinner table. They bless their daughters by saying, "May you be like Sarah, Rebecca, Rachel, and Leah [the matriarchs]." They bless their sons by saying, "May you be like Ephraim and Menashe [two of Jacob's grandchildren]."

Parents then often recite to their children the priestly blessing: "May God bless you and protect you. May God's glory shine upon you. May God be kind and gracious to you and grant you peace."

Some parents include a few personal words after reciting the priestly blessing, and some children offer their parents a blessing in return.

After the wine, dinner begins. In Judaism, meals traditionally start with a blessing over bread, and Shabbat dinner is no exception. Because this meal is no ordinary meal, however, the bread we eat is no ordinary bread. It is made from a rich, golden dough braided as if it were a bride's hair, and brushed with egg or honey. It is called ḥallah.

Some people don't cut the ḥallah with a knife; instead, they tear it with their hands as a reminder that Shabbat is a time of peace, a time when we dream that the nations of the world will put aside their weapons of war forever.

In keeping with the richness of the meal, it is a custom to place not one but two loaves of ḥallah on the table. The rabbis of old teach that the two loaves remind us of the miracle that happened in the Sinai wilderness long ago. After the Exodus, when the Israelites were wandering in the wilderness, food was scarce and the people were hungry. They complained to God, who responded by giving them the gift of manna to eat. Manna was found on the ground six days a week, under the morning dew. The people were told to gather only as much as they could eat on one day. Any excess would spoil.

No manna fell on Shabbat, however. What was to be done? God caused an extra portion of manna to fall on Friday and commanded the Israelites to collect two days' worth. That extra amount did not spoil. As a reminder of how God fed our ancestors in the desert and how the manna fell in double portions in honor of Shabbat, we begin the Shabbat meal with a double portion of ḥallah.

Some families tear ḥallah rather than cut it with a knife, for a knife is associated with weapons of war and on Shabbat we seek to be at peace.

The meal ends with blessings and song. Poets throughout the ages have composed songs about the pleasures of Shabbat, the food, the peace, the joy. With nowhere to rush to and no work calling us away, family and friends sing these songs, sharing new tunes and letting their spirits rise.

What Do You Think?

Some families have a Friday-night-at-home rule. Every member of the family makes a pledge that no matter what—a dance, a party, a meeting—everyone will stay home on Friday night, unless the entire family is invited to celebrate Shabbat with others.

Do you think this rule would work in your home? Why or why not?

_____

_____

_____

What practices do you think your family might observe to celebrate Shabbat on Friday night?

_____

_____

_____

To Prom or Not to Prom

Not long ago, two high school students—Amanda Martin and Rachel Martin (they're not related)—from New York wanted to go to their school prom, but not on a Friday night! So what did they do? They organized an alternative prom, complete with a DJ and buffet dinner, to be held on a Sunday night for juniors and seniors who are members of the Conservative movement's youth group, United Synagogue Youth (USY).

"A lot of USYers won't go to their proms because they are on Shabbat and are at *treif* [nonkosher] places," explained 17-year-old Amanda. "So we decided to hold our own."

Armed with determination, energy, and a list of 550 USY high school juniors and seniors, the two teens publicized and organized the event like pros. Their reward? They and their friends were able both to observe Shabbat *and* to have the time of their lives at the prom!

Shabbat Day

On Shabbat morning the synagogue awaits. As with *kabbalat Shabbat,* the morning prayers speak of God's greatness and the majesty of Creation. The centerpiece of the service is the Torah reading. All personal celebrations happen around it; all prayers for healing are woven through it; the sermon or *d'var Torah* is linked to it. Every week, one *parashah* is chanted from the Torah scroll, just as it was centuries ago.

On Shabbat, seven people are traditionally given the honor of sharing in the Torah reading, although most don't actually read. One by one they are called up to the *bimah.* This going up to the *bimah* is called an *aliyah.* Those honored with an *aliyah* recite a blessing before and after the reading of their section of the *parashah.*

Just as the most social part of Friday-night services is the *oneg Shabbat,* so, in many synagogues, the most social part of Shabbat-morning services is the *kiddush.* After the services, everyone gathers around tables of food and drink. The blessings over the day, over the wine and, often, over the ḥallah are recited. And people shmooze.

At the end of the Torah service, the scroll is lifted up for the entire community to see. This ritual is called hagbahah.

After the morning services, people may continue on to a bat or bar mitzvah meal and celebration, or they may return home to eat lunch, read, take walks, or perhaps play pickup games of basketball or football. They may go to a park or visit a friend, or enjoy some other leisure activity. In keeping with the Shabbat tradition of *bikkur holim*—visiting the sick—some synagogues arrange for their members to visit patients in nearby hospitals or nursing homes.

A light late-afternoon meal, called a *se'udah shlishit* (third meal), completes the formal eating for the day.

Imagine that you are a member of your synagogue's hospitality committee. Think about how you can make your synagogue a warmer, friendlier place on Shabbat. For example, how might you help welcome new members and visitors to your synagogue? How might you encourage families to celebrate Shabbat with others, sharing what they know and love of this holy day? How might you encourage families as well as those who live alone to reach out to others, including the elderly, by inviting guests for dinner on *erev Shabbat*?

_____

_____

_____

_____

_____

_____

_____

_____

_____

TAKING ACTION: FAMILY PEACE

On Shabbat we leave behind the tensions of the week so that shalom—peace—can fill the day. We can help bring family peace, or *sh'lom bayit,* to our homes by showing respect to our parents and exercising patience with our brothers and sisters.

The *midrash* Avot de Rabbi Natan explains: "Those who make peace in their homes are as if they made peace in all Israel." What can you do to help make your home a more peaceful and loving place?

_____

_____

_____

_____

_____

By first learning to live peaceably with those we love, we can establish an island of shalom that slowly extends beyond the confines of our homes.

Havdalah

After the sun sets, when three medium-size stars can be seen in the sky, Shabbat ends. It is escorted out with a special service called *havdalah* (separation). Just as we entered the sacred space of Shabbat through a doorway of candlelight, so too do we leave it. With a cup of wine, a container of spices, and a lighted, long, braided candle, *havdalah* leads the way back to the workaday world that awaits us.

Back to the Sources

The first ritual of *havdalah* begins when we raise the cup of wine and recite the blessing over wine without drinking. We then place the cup back on the table and recite the blessing over spices:

בָּרוּךְ אַתָּה, יְיָ אֱלֹהֵינוּ, מֶלֶךְ הָעוֹלָם, בּוֹרֵא מִינֵי בְשָׂמִים.

Blessed are you, Adonai our God, Sovereign of the universe, who creates all kinds of spices.

We pass the spice container around and inhale the scent of the spices. Then we recite the blessing over the *havdalah* candle as we raise our hands, noticing the light of the flame through our fingernails and the play of shadow and light on our hands:

בָּרוּךְ אַתָּה, יְיָ אֱלֹהֵינוּ, מֶלֶךְ הָעוֹלָם, בּוֹרֵא מְאוֹרֵי הָאֵשׁ.

Blessed are You, Adonai our God, Sovereign of the universe, who creates the light of fire.

The blessing of separation begins:

בָּרוּךְ אַתָּה, יְיָ אֱלֹהֵינוּ, מֶלֶךְ הָעוֹלָם, הַמַּבְדִּיל בֵּין קֹדֶשׁ לְחֹל, בֵּין אוֹר לְחֹשֶׁךְ.

Blessed are You, Adonai our God, Sovereign of the universe, who separates the holy from the ordinary, the light from the darkness.

A sip of wine is taken and the candle is extinguished in the remaining wine.

Havdalah *set—a spice container, Kiddush cup, and candleholder*

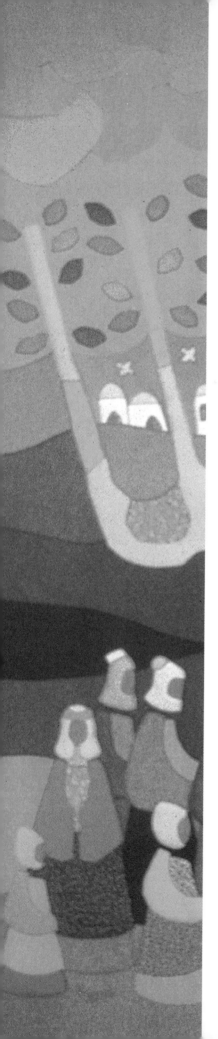

Our rest is over. We return to where we left off. School work needs to be done; garbage needs to be taken out; our clothes need to be washed. With God at our side, we work for another six days until the next Shabbat, when we reenter God's palace in time.

A Tradition of iNNoVāTion

Because *havdalah* is a time of separation, some Jews are using it to mark personal transitions. For example, rituals for a child going off to camp or college, and for families seeking healing after a divorce or serious illness, are being woven into the symbols of *havdalah*. Just as *havdalah* distinguishes Shabbat from the workweek, so these rituals are designed to help families and friends cope with other separations in their lives.

Describe a ritual based on *havdalah* that you might create for the occasion of a friend moving to another state or going off to camp. Which elements of *havdalah* would you want to include, and what new words or rituals would you want to add?

_____

_____

_____

_____

_____

_____

_____

_____

_____

_____

_____

_____

_____

_____

_____

_____

HONORING AND CREATING JEWISH TRADITION

- What do you think is the most important message or lesson of Shabbat? Describe one way this teaching can help you become your best self.

  _____

  _____

  _____

  _____

- Describe a traditional Shabbat ritual or custom that you particularly enjoy, and explain why you enjoy it.

  _____

  _____

  _____

- How can you add beauty and meaning to Shabbat through the tradition of *hiddur mitzvah*?

  _____

  _____

- Describe a new ritual (or an innovation to a familiar ritual) that you would like to add to the traditions of Shabbat. Explain why this addition would be appropriate and how it would add meaning or beauty to Shabbat.

  _____

  _____

  _____

  _____

  _____

This tapestry, titled "Thou Shall Keep the Sabbath," is by Lydie Egosi.

CHAPTER 8

ראשׁ חֹדֶשׁ

ROSH ḤODESH
New Moon, New Month

*God, grant us a long and peaceful life,
a life of goodness and blessing, a life of
achievement and strength of body, a life
of decency and dignity, free from shame
and full of honor, a life filled with Torah
and love for You.*

—from the blessing announcing the New Moon

*A waning moon
right before
Rosh Ḥodesh*

Each month of the Jewish calendar has its own personality. Some months are joyous, like Adar, which is buoyed by the humor and feasting of Purim's celebration. Some are subdued, for example, Ḥeshvan, which has no holiday at all except for the semi-holiday of Rosh Ḥodesh. Some are bittersweet, like Nisan, the month in which both Passover and Yom Hashoah occur, for we remember not only the joy of our delivery from slavery in ancient Egypt, but also the tragic loss of six million Jewish lives in modern times.

But no matter what celebrations or losses mark a month, Rosh Ḥodesh—the first day of the month—is always joyous and inspiring. It reminds us that life is always full of new possibilities and new beginnings, new opportunities and new adventures.

The Measure of Time

Besides serving as a symbol of renewal, the moon has also played a practical role for the Jews, as an instrument for keeping time. Tracking the changes in the moon's monthly cycle was the central way in which our ancestors measured the length of months.

Two thousand years ago there was no published Jewish calendar. The arrival of the New Moon—the first sliver of light to be seen after the old moon fades completely—had to be witnessed before the new month could be declared. Given the moon's rotation around the earth, the new month could begin on either the thirtieth or the thirty-first day after the previous New Moon. Knowing of this uncertainty, the Jewish people would await the official declaration of the New Moon.

Keeping the calendar was a sacred task because knowing when to observe the holidays depended upon it. During the Second Temple period, calculating the calendar was one of the major responsibilities of the Sanhedrin, the Jewish supreme court located in Jerusalem. Only through the Sanhedrin's declarations did the Jews in Israel know when to gather for the Passover seder, when to sit in the sukkah, when to mark the New Year of the Trees.

How did the members of this high court know when the new month began? On the 30th day of the month, they would sit in session in a courtyard in Jerusalem and wait for testimony to be presented. Witnesses who had seen the light of the New Moon would run to the Sanhedrin to announce it. They would be questioned by the court about the color of the moon, its height in the sky, the direction the arc of light faced, and more. If the judges were satisfied that the testimony of at least two of the witnesses was reliable, they would declare that the month had been 29 days, and the new month had begun.

A shofar would be blown, and bonfires were lit from mountaintop to mountaintop to let people far and wide know that the

What Do You Think?

Any people who wants to remain united needs a common calendar and a common timekeeper so that everyone shows up at the same time for activities such as school, celebration, prayer, and voting. Today the world is united by Greenwich mean time. In the biblical and Talmudic periods, the Jews set their calendars by Sanhedrin time.

What value do you think there is to the Jewish people's continuing to have their own calendar?

_____

_____

New Moon and the new month had been proclaimed. If there were not at least two reliable witnesses, or if the evening was cloudy, the New Moon was declared for the following day. Later on, the Sanhedrin created a system of runners to alert people.

Those who lived outside that circle of communication would observe Rosh Ḥodesh on the 30th day of the month. That method of declaration continued until the middle of the 4th century, when the rabbis established a permanent calendar.

How We Celebrate

From the earliest of times, Rosh Ḥodesh has been celebrated as a semiholiday. In the biblical period, feasts would be held, and women, especially, would seek out the prophets for advice and help. Today it is celebrated as a day of joy. Rosh Ḥodesh is a time for new beginnings, a time to test new skills, and to dare to make changes in our lives. Some people set Rosh Ḥodesh as the day to begin new activities, such as hobbies, extracurricular sports or studies, or taking better care of their health.

The celebration of Rosh Ḥodesh begins the week before the new moon and continues up to 14 days afterward. The Shabbat before Rosh Ḥodesh is called Shabbat Mevorchim, the Sabbath of Blessing. After the Torah reading, the congregation rises. The cantor, or whoever is leading the service, holds the Torah and chants a special blessing (a portion of which is found at the beginning of this chapter) on behalf of the congregation and the entire people of Israel. It is a prayer of hope and the power to overcome fear. A proclamation is then made, telling everyone when the new moon will appear, down to the very hour. The congregation repeats the proclamation to reinforce the news.

In honor of the semiholiday of Rosh Ḥodesh we read Numbers 28:9–15 from the Torah. (When Rosh Ḥodesh falls on Shabbat, we read these verses as a supplement to the regular weekly portion. A

כי
קרוב
אליך
הדבר
מאד
בפיך
ובלבבך
לעשתו

This Torah mantle by Peachy Levy is called "In Gratitude to God." On Rosh Hodesh we express our gratitude to God by reciting the psalms of Hallel. How can celebrating Rosh Hodesh strengthen you by reminding you of the good in your life?

special *haftarah*, Isaiah 66:1–24, which speaks of hope and rebirth, replaces the *haftarah* that would otherwise be chanted after the reading of the *parashah* for that Shabbat.) Hallel, the psalms of praise and rejoicing, is recited. Tefillin, or phylacteries—the black boxes and leather straps that Jews wrap around their arms and heads during weekday-morning blessings—are removed for the latter part of the morning prayers as a sign of the New Moon's holiday status, for tefillin are not worn on holidays.

As a class, you can check a Jewish calendar and study verses of Hallel in preparation for Rosh Ḥodesh.

Back to the Sources

Hallel, a series of psalms praising God, is recited during the morning service on Passover, Sukkot, Shavuot, Ḥanukkah, Yom Yerushalayim, and Yom Ha'atzma'ut, as well as on Rosh Ḥodesh. The name Hallel comes from the first word in Psalm 113, *halleluyah,* which means "praise God."

הַלְלוּיָה הַלְלוּ עַבְדֵי יְיָ הַלְלוּ אֶת־שֵׁם יְיָ:

יְהִי שֵׁם יְיָ מְבֹרָךְ מֵעַתָּה וְעַד־עוֹלָם:

Halleluyah! Give praise, you who serve Adonai, praise the name of Adonai.
Blessed be the name of Adonai from now and for eternity. (Psalm 113:1–2)

Hallel is made up of Psalms 113–118.

Rosh Ḥodesh is a holiday for everyone, but women have a special attachment to the day. For at least 2,000 years, Jewish women have celebrated the arrival of the New Moon in their own way—by not doing such work as sewing, spinning, weaving, or needlework. In the past, Rosh Ḥodesh was a day on which women were free of family chores, a one- or two-day vacation they honored every month. In some communities, women would come together to light candles (perhaps recalling the bonfires of Israel), tell one another stories, and enjoy one another's company.

The rabbis offered the following explanation for the special relationship between women and the New Moon: After the Exodus, while Moses was on Mount Sinai receiving the Torah from God, the Israelites, impatient and worried that he would not return, constructed an idol. They pooled their gold and made the Golden Calf. But in this case, the rabbis tell us, "Israelites" means only the men. The women would not participate; they refused to offer up their gold and jewelry to make an idol. Yet when the time was right, they proved themselves generous, for when Moses returned and the building of the Tabernacle began, they gave generously of their prized belongings to help make the sacred instruments of the Temple. The rabbis taught that God rewarded the women for their faith and generosity by giving Rosh Ḥodesh to them as their holiday.

A Tradition of iNNoVāTion

Just as Moses led the men of Israel out of Egypt, so did Miriam the prophet, Moses' sister, lead the women. Upon crossing the Sea of Reeds, she chanted for them, "Sing to Adonai, for God has triumphed gloriously," and led them in a dance of victory.

Today, as a reminder of Miriam and other remarkable Jewish women throughout the ages, some women buy or create a special cup of Miriam for use during their Rosh Ḥodesh celebrations.

Name two remarkable Jewish women—from the Bible, such as the matriarchs, or from modern times, such as Golda Meir, fourth prime minister of Israel, and Ruth Bader Ginsberg, United States Supreme Court justice—whose lives you would want to honor and explain why.

_____

_____

_____

_____

These cups of Miriam by Linda Gissen, Linda Leviton, and Norma Minkowitz, were made using a variety of materials—bronze, glass, enamel, copper, and clay.

Today, either alone or together in synagogues, JCCs, and one another's homes, women around the world celebrate Rosh Ḥodesh in a variety of ways. They light scented candles, sing, share stories, study Torah, and enjoy the pleasures of a good meal.

ONE PEOPLE, MANY CUSTOMS:
Foods for Rosh Ḥodesh

Women who gather in celebration of Rosh Ḥodesh often bring foods that are symbolic of new beginnings, wholeness, and hope: lentil soup or salad, bagels or other round breads, nuts and fruit, cheese wheels, and hard-boiled eggs.

TAKING ACTION: HOPE

Jewish tradition stresses the importance of hope, for without hope we could not take the actions that help us meet life's challenges. In fact, the unofficial national anthem of the Jewish people's homeland, Israel, is called *Hatikvah*, which means "The Hope."

Consider what challenge you would feel strong enough to take on if only you felt hopeful that you could succeed. Perhaps you want to learn a new skill or do volunteer work. After selecting a challenge, write a blessing asking God to renew and strengthen your hope on Rosh Ḥodesh.

_____

_____

_____

_____

_____

_____

Olive branches are a symbol of peace as well as hope. Eating Israeli olives on Rosh Ḥodesh reminds us of our hope for peace in the Land of Israel and for all Creation.

Light Bulbs: Sharing Your Bright Ideas

Imagine that you are a member of your synagogue's ritual committee. Outline a Rosh Ḥodesh celebration that helps mark the day as a time of joy, hope, and renewal. For example, you might create a celebration in which participants recite psalms from Hallel and sing songs that express peace and hope, such as *Oseh Shalom* and *Lo Yisa Goy*. You might also want to include time for silent prayers or meditation.

_____

_____

_____

_____

_____

_____

Share your ideas with your classmates and together plan a celebration for your class, school, or synagogue for the next Rosh Ḥodesh.

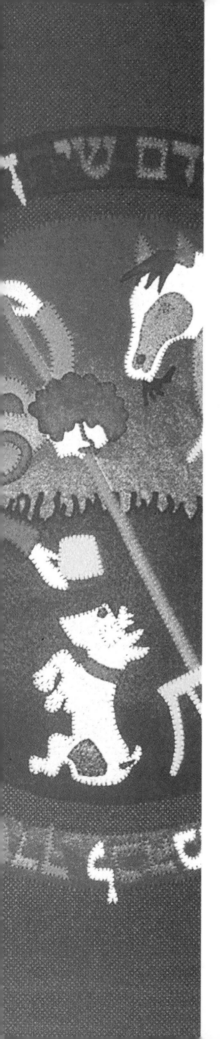

The celebration of Rosh Ḥodesh—for both men and women—continues with the *kiddush halevanah*, the sanctification of the New Moon, on the first or second Saturday night of the month. After the evening service, if the skies are clear and the moon can be seen, the congregation goes outdoors. Congregants turn to the sky and recite the following: "*Halleluyah*. Praise God from the heavens, praise God from the heights. . . . Blessed are You, Adonai our God, Sovereign of the universe, who with but a word created the heavens and who said to the moon that she will be renewed as a crown of splendor for all God's children, just as they are destined to be renewed like her."

This 1682 etching shows a Jewish community celebrating the renewal of the moon.

HONORING AND CREATING JEWISH TRADITION

- What do you think is the most important message or lesson of Rosh Ḥodesh? Describe one way this teaching can help you become your best self.

  _____

  _____

  _____

  _____

- Describe a traditional Rosh Ḥodesh ritual or custom that you think is particularly meaningful, and explain why you find meaning in it.

  _____

  _____

  _____

- How can you add beauty and meaning to Rosh Ḥodesh through the tradition of *hiddur mitzvah*?

  _____

  _____

- Describe a new ritual (or an innovation to a familiar ritual) that you would like to add to the traditions of Rosh Ḥodesh. Explain why this addition would be appropriate and how it would add meaning or beauty to Rosh Ḥodesh.

  _____

  _____

  _____

  _____

  _____

  _____

How might tracking the phases of the moon help us become more focused on nature and our responsibilities as caretakers of Creation? This wall hanging by Naomi Hordes, "Care for Other Living Creatures," includes quotes from the Talmud and Bible about caring for animals.

CHAPTER 9

חֲנֻכָּה

ḤANUKKAH

Rededicating Ourselves

25 Kislev–2 Tevet

These candles that we light are reminders of the miracles and wonders, the salvation and the battles that You won for our ancestors . . . and on all these eight days of Ḥanukkah, these candles are holy; we are not to read by them or work by them; we are, quite simply, to admire them.

—words recited or sung when lighting the Ḥanukkah candles

For eight nights, the glow of Ḥanukkah candles fills our lives with hope and wonder.

W hat makes you proud to be a citizen of this country? How do you show your pride and dedication? Do you march in parades that celebrate national heroes or holidays? get together with family on Thanksgiving? sing the national anthem? observe the laws of the land?

What makes you proud to be a Jew, a partner in our holy Covenant with God? And how do you show your pride and dedication? Do you study Torah? celebrate Shabbat and Yom Ha'atzma'ut? sing Hebrew songs? observe God's mitzvot?

Do you think it is possible to be both a good Jew *and* a good citizen? Why or why not?

Louis Brandeis, the first Jewish United States Supreme Court justice (serving from 1916–1939) and a leading Zionist figure, proved that it is possible to be a dedicated Jew and also be a good citizen—in fact, a leader—of the United States. However, Jews have not always had the freedom to observe our religion, and even today there are places where we are not permitted to do so. The holiday of Ḥanukkah celebrates our people's spirit and determination to live freely as Jews.

Historical Background

In the year 167 BCE, Israel was ruled by a Syrian king named Antiochus Epiphanes (Antiochus IV), who believed himself worthy of worship. Jealous of the Jews' loyalty to the God of Israel, Antiochus banned the practice of Judaism in his kingdom. He forbade Jews to circumcise their sons, learn Hebrew, study the Torah, keep their calendar, observe their holidays, or offer sacrifices in the Temple. Instead, as a Hellenist—one committed to the ancient Greek culture and religion—he commanded the Jews to sacrifice to the Greek gods. His other subjects did, he said, and Jews should, too.

Young Jewish men were expected to study philosophy, mathematics, and science. They were to read the finest of Greek plays and develop an appreciation for the best of Greek culture, including the value of physical beauty. Most important, they were to give up their "mistaken" ways of Judaism.

To ensure that his decree would be obeyed and that all Jews would reject the tradition of their ancestors, Antiochus desecrated the Holy Temple, the center of Jewish life. He captured Jerusalem and made his own sacrifices in the Temple. In place of the holy altar, the sacrifices, and the prayers of generations of Jews, Antiochus set up a statue of Zeus, the chief god of the Greeks. Pigs were sacrificed there, an act that symbolized the Temple's ruin and desecration. Antiochus believed that he had defeated the God of Israel. With the Temple desecrated, the Jews' ruling class

What Do You Think?

The priests of ancient Israel had the job of lighting the Temple's seven-branched menorah. But today there is no more Temple. Our homes have symbolically replaced the Temple, and we have become the priests. "The stones of the ruined Temple were scattered around the world," a *midrash* tells us. Wherever the stones fell, a place of holiness was built: a synagogue, a school, a home. Our homes are symbols of the Temple that stood so long ago.

Do you think your synagogue is a holy place? Why or why not?

_____

_____

Do you think your religious school is a holy place? Why or why not?

_____

_____

Do you think your home is a holy place? Why or why not?

_____

_____

converting to the ways of Hellenism, and their political structures overrun, Jews could no longer continue to be Jews. They would, thought Antiochus, now become Greeks. And many did.

Still other Jews, called zealots, were extremists who shut themselves off from the attraction of Hellenism. They closed their ears and eyes, rejecting even those things that would enrich their lives and their understanding of God's world. They rejected *all* Hellenizing influences and followed none but the strictest of Jewish practices. When the Greeks attacked on Shabbat, the zealots chose not to defend themselves, because that would desecrate Shabbat. Many of them died.

Most Jews, however, neither rejected Judaism, nor sought out Hellenism. And they did not choose to die. Instead, they outwardly embraced the visible symbols of Hellenism—for example, building altars to the Greek gods outside their homes—yet remained faithful to Judaism in their hearts.

One day a group of Syrian soldiers came to the town of Modi'in, just northwest of Jerusalem. They built an altar to force the Jews to demonstrate publicly their loyalty to Zeus and Antiochus. There lived in Modi'in a dedicated Jewish family known as the Hasmoneans: Mattathias and his five sons. They wanted to prevent the Syrians from winning over more Jews. And they wanted to retake the Temple and rededicate it to God.

When the Syrian soldiers gathered the Jews into the middle of the town, one of the Jews accepted their call to come forward to bow down before the altar that had been built. Mattathias stepped forward and killed him. Knowing this was a declaration of war, Mattathias turned to the Jews around him and said, "Let all who choose God follow me."

Mattathias slaying a Jew who abandoned Judaism

TAKING ACTION: DEDICATING OURSELVES TO JEWISH TRADITION

Ḥanukkah means "dedication." *Ḥanukkat habayit* means "dedication of the home." Traditionally, when a family moves into a new home they invite friends and family to a *ḥanukkat habayit*, at which time they hang a mezuzah on the doorposts.

A mezuzah is a sign of our commitment to Jewish traditions and beliefs. It is made up of a case and a small piece of parchment on which is written the Sh'ma prayer and one other passage from the Torah. The text says that God gave us the mitzvah of studying Torah. The parchment is rolled up and placed inside the case.

When a new family joins your community or a new student joins your class, how can you be welcoming?

_____

_____

What actions can you take to show that you are dedicated to the Jewish values that help make us caring people?

_____

_____

Not only is it a tradition to affix a mezuzah to the doorway of a home, it is also appropriate to affix one to the doorway of an office, store, or other place of business.

For three years Mattathias and his sons led the Jews in battles against the Syrians. In the beginning, the Jewish army was small. The soldiers hid in caves and fought in small bands. They gathered faithful recruits from town to town. As their number grew, so did their power. Soon they fought in open battle.

Mattathias was old and he died during the war. His son Judah Maccabee rose to take his place. Under Judah, the Jewish army led successful guerrilla attacks against the Syrians. After winning many smaller victories, the Maccabees waged and won the most important battle of all: the fight for Jerusalem.

Having regained control of Jerusalem, the Jews immediately went to the Temple and destroyed the statue of Zeus. They took apart the altar upon which Greek sacrifices had been made. They cleaned out the halls and the courtyards and rededicated the Temple to God and the Jewish people. That is how Ḥanukkah got its name, for Ḥanukkah means "dedication."

Legend has it that when the Jews began to clean the Temple, they found just one small container of consecrated olive oil, the only kind that could be burned in the Temple. There was enough oil to burn for only one day, but the restorations and the manufacture of new oil would take at least a week. Still, the Jews lit that little bit of oil.

To everyone's wonder, it lasted for eight days and eight nights. Its flame went out only when the new oil was ready. From that time to this day, we say that a great miracle happened there, and sing the words in a song.

ONE PEOPLE, MANY CUSTOMS:
Holiday Foods

In America, the traditional Ḥanukkah food is potato latkes—pancakes. Some families also make latkes from cheese or from vegetables such as zucchini and carrots. We eat latkes because of the oil used in the frying, which reminds us of the miracle of the oil. In Israel, the traditional Ḥanukkah food is doughnuts, called *sufganiot.* They are fried in oil too, and likewise remind us of the miracle of the oil. Many Sephardic Jews use oil to fry other pastries that are then dipped in sweet syrup.

The sixth night of Ḥanukkah is also Rosh Ḥodesh, the New Moon. On this night, Jews from Morocco traditionally eat a festive dairy meal that includes sweet couscous, which is made with dried fruits and nuts and may be served with buttermilk or yogurt. On the last day of Ḥanukkah, many Turkish Jews invite friends and relatives to a special meal called *merenda*— a potluck meal in which each guest brings a dish to share with everyone.

What foods do you like to eat on Ḥanukkah?

_____

_____

Peeling and grating potatoes is best done by a duo. Frying latkes is a one-person job. But when it comes to eating latkes, the more eaters the merrier—as long as the latkes hold out!

Back to the Sources

The ancient rabbis chose a *haftarah* portion that would remind the Jewish people that God—not humans—was responsible for the victory of the Maccabees. On the Shabbat of Ḥanukkah, we read from the Book of Zechariah:

$$\text{...לֹא בְחַיִל וְלֹא בְכֹחַ כִּי אִם־בְּרוּחִי אָמַר יְיָ צְבָאוֹת:}$$

"*. . . Not by might nor by power but by My Spirit,*" *says* Adonai Tzva'ot, *the Lord of Hosts.*

(Zechariah 4:6)

How We Celebrate

Although Ḥanukkah is not mentioned in the Bible, the writers of the Talmud noted it by debating the laws of lighting the candles. "What time of day is appropriate for lighting the *ḥanukkiyah* [Ḥanukkah menorah]?" they asked. "Should you light eight candles the first night and decrease the number every night thereafter, like the lessening of the oil, or should you light one candle the first night and increase the number every night thereafter, like the growing wonder of the miracle?" The answer is given in the Talmud, *Shabbat* 21a: It is best to light the candles at nightfall, when the last customers are leaving the market. Light one candle the first night, and increase the number every night thereafter, for we choose to celebrate the growing sense of wonder and not its decrease.

A Tradition of iNNoVãTion

Like Simḥat Torah, Ḥanukkah is not mentioned in the Bible. In fact, Ḥanukkah was declared a holiday by the Maccabees themselves to mark their victory.

The Maccabees determined that Ḥanukkah should begin on the 25th of Kislev, last for eight days (some think that the number was chosen as a reenactment of the holidays of Sukkot and Shemini Atzeret, which the Maccabees were unable to celebrate during the war), and involve lights. At the time, declaring a Jewish holiday that was not mentioned in the Bible was a daring innovation. Since that time, there have been many additions to the Jewish calendar, for example, new holidays such as Tu B'Shevat, Yom Ha'atzma'ut, Yom Hazikaron, Yom Yerushalayim, and Yom Hashoah.

The Ḥanukkah candlelighting proclaims the miracle of the Temple's restoration. Therefore, each *ḥanukkiyah*—designed to resemble the seven-branched menorah of the Temple but with eight branches to symbolize the eight days of Ḥanukkah (plus one extra for the *shammash,* the helper)—is to be placed on a window sill for all to see.

In times past, when it was not safe for us to show our pride in being Jewish and celebrate openly, we were encouraged to light our candles away from the windows. But today we are free, and our living room windowsills are perfect places for lighting candles and commemorating the miracle of Ḥanukkah for all to see.

In the United States, Ḥanukkah is seen as part of America's great tradition of inclusiveness and diversity. In 1996, a postage stamp was created with a ḥanukkiyah on it, expressing America's respect for Jews and Judaism.

There are two blessings that we recite as we light the Ḥanukkah candles. The first is over the candles themselves: "Blessed are You, Adonai our God, Sovereign of the universe, who has sanctified us through Your mitzvot and commands us to light the Ḥanukkah lights." The second is over the miracle: "Blessed are You, Adonai our God, Sovereign of the universe, who worked miracles for our ancestors in those days at this very time of year."

This second blessing says miracles, *nissim,* instead of miracle, *nes.* Tradition has identified two miracles of Ḥanukkah: one military, one supernatural. Perhaps, there is a third miracle of Ḥanukkah: that throughout the ages we Jews have managed to weave the ways of the world—its architecture, clothing, food, and languages—into Judaism without losing our identity, our purpose, or our Covenant with God. The Hasmoneans understood that living a Jewishly committed life is not all or nothing, that you can adapt to some of the outside culture and still remain a dedicated Jew. Their grandchildren's names prove the point: Hyrcanus, for example, is a Greek name.

And on the first night of the holiday, we add the Sheheḥeyanu, the blessing that is recited at the beginning of every celebration.

How to Light the Ḥanukkah Candles

Put the candles in the menorah, starting from the right, one candle for each day of Ḥanukkah up to the present night. Then, add one more candle in the place reserved for the *shammash,* the extra candle that is the helper. Since we are not allowed to use the Ḥanukkah candles for anything but celebration and decoration, we light the candles using the *shammash.*

Once the *shammash* is lit, the blessings are recited. The candles are then lit, beginning with the newest candle on the left and moving right toward the candle representing the first day.

Ḥanukkah candles are like Shabbat candles in that we let them burn out by themselves. On *erev Shabbat,* the evening we welcome Shabbat, we light the Ḥanukkah candles first, and then the Shabbat candles. At *havdalah,* when Shabbat is over, we light the *havdalah* candle first and then the Ḥanukkah candles. We do so because of the law that prohibits lighting fire on Shabbat.

On what day of Ḥanukkah was this picture taken? How do you know?

Back to the Sources

In addition to lighting candles, we recite Hallel, the special collection of holiday psalms, every morning of Ḥanukkah and add a prayer to the blessings of the Amidah. The addition to the Amidah recounts the story of Ḥanukkah:

...כְּשֶׁעָמְדָה מַלְכוּת יָוָן הָרְשָׁעָה עַל עַמְּךָ יִשְׂרָאֵל,

לְהַשְׁכִּיחָם תּוֹרָתֶךָ וּלְהַעֲבִירָם מֵחֻקֵּי רְצוֹנֶךָ,

וְאַתָּה, בְּרַחֲמֶיךָ הָרַבִּים, עָמַדְתָּ לָהֶם בְּעֵת צָרָתָם

רַבְתָּ אֶת רִיבָם ...מָסַרְתָּ גִבּוֹרִים בְּיַד חַלָּשִׁים...

. . . when the cruel Greek kingdom rose against the Jews, to force them to forget God's Torah and abandon God's ways, and how You, God, in Your kindness and mercy, stood with the Jews in their time of distress and fought their fight . . . delivering the strong into the arms of the weak. . . .

Sometimes, Jewish prayer is a form of holy storytelling.

Where It Will Stop No One Knows

While the letters on the dreidel can have several meanings, usually the *nun* stands for *nisht*, Yiddish for "nothing"; the one who spun neither gives nor gets anything. *Gimmel* stands for *ganz*, Yiddish for "all"; the spinner takes everything in the pot. *Hay* stands for *halb*, Yiddish for "half"; the spinner takes half the pot. *Shin* stands for *shtell*, Yiddish for "put"; the spinner adds one to the pot.

During the past 100 years, the most popular ways to celebrate Ḥanukkah have been playing with a dreidel (a four-sided top called a *sevivon* in Hebrew), eating nuts as a treat, and receiving a bit of Ḥanukkah *gelt* ("money" in Yiddish).

On each side of the dreidel is a letter indicating one word of the saying *Nes gadol hayah sham,* meaning "A great miracle happened there." "There" refers to Israel, and "a great miracle" refers to the rededication of the Temple. (In Israel they say, *Nes gadol hayah* po, meaning "A great miracle happened *here*.") Each player spins the dreidel in turn. The letter that appears face up indicates what the player is to do—for example, add a penny (or other item, such as a raisin) to the pot or scoop up the pot's contents.

Developing a personal spinning technique is part of the holiday fun. For example, some players begin their spins on a solid surface, while others begin midair and let the dreidel drop.

Which dreidel indicates that the spinner should take everything in the pot?

Light Bulbs: Sharing Your Bright Ideas

Imagine that you are a member of your synagogue's hospitality committee. Create a proposal for pairing new members of the synagogue with more established families who will invite the new members to their homes for candlelighting and latkes or a meal sometime during the eight days of Ḥanukkah. Alternatively, you may want to write a proposal to create a special service for the Shabbat of Ḥanukkah to welcome and honor new members of your congregation.

Be sure to describe why such an activity would be important and to outline what should be done.

_____

_____

_____

_____

_____

_____

_____

_____

_____

A Tradition of iNNoVāTion

Some Jews are beginning to make the eighth day of Ḥanukkah a special day of giving. Instead of getting yet another pair of gloves, they give a pair to the homeless. Instead of getting still another toy, they give one to the children's ward of a local hospital. Instead of getting Ḥanukkah *gelt,* they may give tzedakah in honor of a friend.

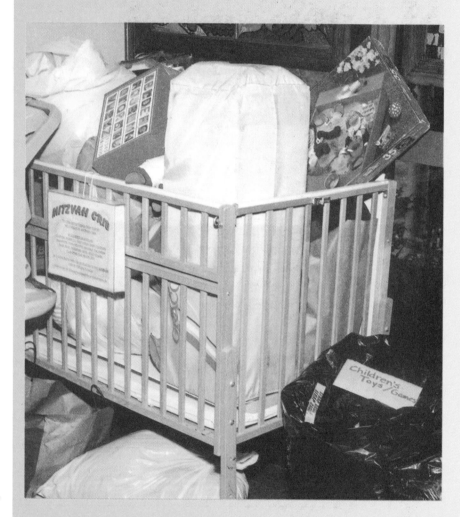

One reward of synagogue membership is being part of a caring community. In many synagogues, holiday celebrations include food, clothing, or toy drives for those in need.

When the last Ḥanukkah candles burn out, the darkness of winter is once again around us. But we have entered a new month, Tevet. The days will begin to lengthen. Spring will soon be here.

HONORING AND CREATING JEWISH TRADITION

- What do you think is the most important message or lesson of Ḥanukkah? Describe one way this teaching can help you become your best self.

  _____

  _____

  _____

  _____

- Describe a traditional Ḥanukkah ritual or custom that you think is particularly meaningful, and explain why you find meaning in it.

  _____

  _____

  _____

- How can you add beauty and meaning to the holiday through the tradition of _hiddur mitzvah_?

  _____

  _____

- Describe a new ritual (or an innovation to a familiar ritual) that you would like to add to the traditions of Ḥanukkah. Explain why this addition would be appropriate and how it would add meaning or beauty to the holiday.

  _____

  _____

  _____

  _____

  _____

  _____

This quilted wall hanging, "Festival of Lights," is by Sheila Groman.

CHAPTER 10

TU B'SHEVAT
Caring for Planet Earth

15 Shevat

> *Rabbi Yoḥanan ben Zakkai said, "If you are holding a seedling in your hand and you hear that the Messiah is coming, plant the seedling and then go and greet the Messiah."*

—Avot de Rabbi Natan

What fruits or vegetables would you miss if there were no plant life on earth?

C an you imagine paradise without trees? Is it any wonder that God chose to put the first people in a garden of trees? "And God planted a garden in Eden . . . and God made to grow from the ground all sorts of trees, pleasant to look at and good for eating" (Genesis 2:8–9). The only task God required of Adam and Eve was to care for the trees.

Trees give us oxygen and forests, paper and wood, flowers and almonds. We could no more live on this earth without trees than we could live without sunshine, air, or water. And because we have the power to plant and destroy trees, Judaism gives us a holiday to celebrate them and remind us of their importance.

Tu B'Shevat is a holiday that calls us outdoors. Most days we live in our houses, which are heated and air conditioned, dashing from home to car to school to extracurricular activites, often ignoring the natural world around us. We live under the heavens all our lives, but most of us can't tell the difference between one type of cloud and another. Living in and around cities, we can hardly see the stars.

Once in a while, however, we feel our loss and try to find ways to return to nature. Tu B'Shevat gives us a way; it reminds us that conserving the earth's natural resources, such as trees, petroleum, and clean air, is a Jewish issue. It reminds us that our lives depend on God's gift of these resources, that some of the resources are renewable and some are not, and that *we* have the power to transform them into the blessings of food and shelter or the curses of pollution. Tu B'Shevat reminds us that we are caretakers, not just consumers, of the earth and its produce.

Orlah and Ma'aser

Tu B'Shevat did not start out as a holiday celebrating the environment. It didn't have special ceremonies or stories to tell or prayers to recite. Originally it was a legal tool for counting the age of a tree, which was important for two reasons: *orlah* and *ma'aser.*

Orlah is the name given to fruit produced during a tree's first three years. According to Jewish law, that fruit may not be eaten or sold. It is set aside, left alone, as a reminder that all food comes from God. The question is, How do we know how old a tree is for the purposes of counting *orlah*? Because a tree may be planted at any time, it would be difficult to remember each tree's age. So Jewish law established the 15th of Shevat as the birthday of all fruit-bearing trees. On the 15th of Shevat, every tree is declared one year older.

Ma'aser, meaning "tenth" in Hebrew, is the name of a particular gift of fruits given to the Temple. Every year, the Jews who lived in Israel had to give a tenth (a tithe) of their new fruits to the

A Jewish folk story tells how Honi was walking along the road when he saw a man planting a carob tree. He asked, "How long before it will bear fruit?"

The man answered, "Seventy years."

Honi asked, "And will you be alive in 70 years to eat from its fruit?"

The man answered, "And what if I am not? Just as I found the world full of carob trees planted by my parents and grandparents, so will I plant for my children" (*Ta'anit* 23a).

What can you do to help ensure that those who come after you will have an abundant, beautiful, and safe environment to live in?

_____

_____

_____

_____

_____

_____

_____

_____

_____

_____

_____

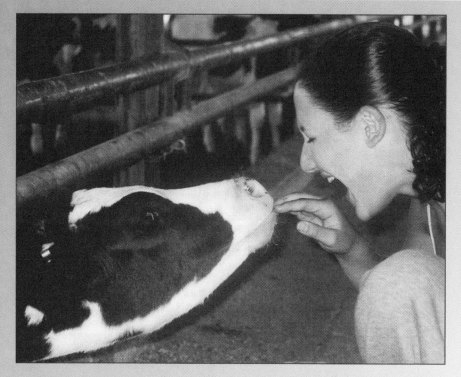

A visit to a farm can focus us on nature's many wonders and delights.

Levites and the priests who worked in the Temple. It was a way to thank God for the rain and the sun and the fertile earth, as well as a way to support the Levites and the priests, who were not permitted to own land or trees.

But the question arose: Given that fruit ripens over a period of time, as a part of which year's harvest should the fruit be counted? The rabbis determined that for the sake of *ma'aser,* the agricultural year would begin on the 15th of Shevat, for by that time the old crop had been harvested. All fruit ripening on and after the 15th of Shevat would be counted as part of the coming year's crop; all fruit that ripened before the 15th of Shevat would be part of the previous year's crop.

After the Temple was destroyed, Jews no longer tithed. Then only *orlah* gave Tu B'Shevat any purpose.

ONE PEOPLE, MANY CUSTOMS:
A Wedding Canopy

A custom reaching back to the Talmudic period suggests that on Tu B'Shevat we plant a cedar for every boy born the previous year and a cypress for every girl. When a man and woman marry, branches from their trees can be cut and used to weave their huppah, their wedding canopy.

What Do You Think?

The Torah tells us that just as we rest every seventh day, the earth must rest every seventh year, meaning that crops should not be planted. This is called the *shemittah* year and is observed by many people in Israel to this day. The land needs time to replenish itself, otherwise its nutrients will dry up and its crops will wither. *Shemittah* also reminds us that we are caretakers, not owners, of the land.

What do you think the difference is between caring for the earth because you want to be a responsible citizen and doing so because it is a mitzvah?

_____

_____

_____

_____

These pomegranates will turn red when they ripen. Pomegranates were grown in ancient Israel and continue to be cultivated in modern Israel. They are mentioned many times in the Bible, along with figs, dates, olives, and grapes.

The Transformation of Tu B'Shevat

Four hundred years ago, a small number of Jews from all around the Mediterranean Sea immigrated to Palestine and settled in the northern town of Safed. These Jews were kabbalists—mystics—who believed that ever since Creation, hidden sparks of holiness had been trapped in the physical world. They believed that before Creation, God had filled the universe entirely, but that to make room for the physical world, God had contracted, moving over to make space for what was about to be created. Yet a physical world without godliness would be an empty shell. God therefore created vessels that could carry the Divine Presence into the physical world. At first, all was fine. But as the flow of holiness increased the vessels burst. The sacred was trapped in all the broken pieces of the vessels. Our task, according to the mystics, is to release those holy sparks and let them reunite with their Source.

We do this, the kabbalists believed, every time we perform a mitzvah, as long as we carry it out with the proper intent. Thus by celebrating Tu B'Shevat in the right way, by attending to the hidden sparks in nature, Jews could release the holiness.

Ḥalutzim *preparing to eat dinner in the fields*

This wall hanging by Naomi Hordes was inspired by the seal of the Moses Montefiore Foundation. The foundation provided funds for the settlement of ḥalutzim and the purchase of land in Israel.

Wanting to use every opportunity to observe this mitzvah, the kabbalists developed a Tu B'Shevat seder, modeled on the Passover seder. They drank four cups of wine, each one darker than the one before—white, pink, rosé, and red. They ate certain kinds of fruits: those whose outsides cannot be eaten (like nuts), those whose insides cannot be eaten (like cherries), and those that can be eaten in their entirety (like raisins).

For many years, the Tu B'Shevat seder was celebrated only by the kabbalists and the holiday was almost lost. Then, in the late 1800s, young European Jews—largely in their teens and twenties, immigrated to Palestine in great numbers. These pioneers, called *ḥalutzim,* came to work the land. They knew that just as they were going to make Israel's deserts, swamp lands, and abandoned fields bloom, so too would the Jewish people bloom once again in *Eretz Yisrael*—the Land of Israel.

The pioneers lived in tents and simple homes. They founded kibbutzim, agricultural and industrial collectives. They planted trees, many of them: trees that drained the swamps which bred malaria, trees that provided shade during the broiling summer days, trees that brought the wastelands of *Eretz Yisrael* back to life.

If Tu B'Shevat had been only a legal device, it might have died out. But the Jews saw in it a greater value: Tu B'Shevat became the emblem of the ḥalutzim. Even in exile, those Jews who lived far from Jerusalem once again began to celebrate their connection to the Land of Israel on the 15th of Shevat. They created rituals and ate the foods of Israel that are mentioned in the Bible: wheat, barley, grapes, figs, pomegranates, olives, dates, honey, carobs, and almonds. A holiday that marked spring's renewal in Israel became a holiday that marks our national renewal.

When you visit Israel, you can plant your own tree!

Back to the Sources

Judaism teaches us that, even in the midst of war, we must not destroy trees:

כִּי־תָצוּר אֶל־עִיר יָמִים רַבִּים לְהִלָּחֵם עָלֶיהָ
לְתָפְשָׂהּ לֹא־תַשְׁחִית אֶת־עֵצָהּ לִנְדֹּחַ עָלָיו גַּרְזֶן
כִּי מִמֶּנּוּ תֹאכֵל וְאֹתוֹ לֹא תִכְרֹת...

When you lay siege to a city for a long time, you may not cut down the trees for you can eat from them; you should not destroy them . . . (Deuteronomy 20:19)

What good is winning, the Torah seems to be asking, if all is destroyed in victory?

How We Celebrate

Expressing the Message of Love of Israel

In 1901, in order to help the *halutzim,* Jewish leadership in the Diaspora created the Jewish National Fund (JNF), an organization dedicated to developing land in Israel and planting trees there. With financial support from JNF and with the pioneering work of the *halutzim, Eretz Yisrael* once again blossomed. JNF chose one day of the year, Tu B'Shevat, as the day on which to focus the attention of Jews around the world on *Eretz Yisrael.*

For decades, on Tu B'Shevat, Israeli children have planted thousands of trees all over the country. Israelis young and old—*olim* (newcomers) and *vatikim* (old-timers), visitors and politicians—plant saplings throughout the countryside. Towns and kibbutzim alike hold special celebrations, their citizens grateful for the Land of Israel, and for the trees that flourish there.

When we plant trees in Israel, we fulfill the words of the Torah: "When you come into the land, you shall plant all kinds of fruit trees. . . . For Adonai, your God, will bring you into a good land, a land with streams and springs and fountains coming forth from plain and hill, a land of wheat and barley and vines and fig trees and pomegranates, a land of olive trees and honey" (Leviticus 19:23; Deuteronomy 8:7).

The elderly and ill often find it healing to plant a seedling and watch it grow. Imagine that you are a member of your synagogue's social justice committee who wants to celebrate Tu B'Shevat by organizing a group to visit a senior citizens' home or a hospital to plant bulbs, such as tulips and amaryllis.

Brainstorm places that might be interested in such project, a list of the materials you will need, such as, pots, bulbs, potting soil, and simple gardening tools, and a way to raise funds to pay for the materials. Then work with others to make this idea into a reality. This can become a synagogue, school, or class event.

_____

_____

_____

_____

_____

_____

_____

_____

_____

_____

_____

_____

_____

Expressing the Message of Environmentalism
Since the 1970s, Tu B'Shevat has served another purpose as well. It has become a holiday on which Jews celebrate the gift of our world—the earth, the seas, and the air—and our responsibility to preserve and care for it. For too many years, people have used the earth's resources carelessly. We have destroyed. We have wasted. We have polluted. Although this is a worldwide problem, not just a Jewish problem, many Jews are turning to Tu B'Shevat as a special day on which to remember that we must work to preserve the world and that we must teach and remind others to do the same.

A Tu B'Shevat Seder or Meal

Like the earlier kabbalists, some Jews today celebrate with a Tu B'Shevat seder at home, synagogue, or religious school. These seders combine the message of love of Israel with respect for the earth. A modest alternative to the seder is a special holiday meal featuring the seven species, or fruits, that symbolize the abundant and fertile Land of Israel. Such a meal could begin with the blessing over wine recited over wine or grape juice from Israel, and continue with round ḥallah, barley soup, fresh salad with olives and olive oil, a vegetarian main course, figs, dates, a pomegranate, and a carob-topped almond cake for dessert.

TAKING ACTION: DO NOT BE WASTEFUL

Do not destroy mindlessly. *Bal tashhit!* That is a basic principle of Judaism. Cutting down rain forests needlessly, polluting the air with harmful smoke, failing to recycle or put out a campfire, wasting water—all deplete and endanger the earth's precious and limited resources.

List two actions you take on a daily basis that show your concern for nature and the environment.

_____

_____

What could you do more (or less) of to help protect our planet?

_____

_____

Thousands of recycling bins, such as this one, are in cities throughout Israel. In one year, approximately one ton of plastic waste is collected in each bin. The plastic is then shredded into confetti-sized pieces, melted down, and recycled into useful products, such as bus stops, park benches, and storage containers.

A Tradition of iNNoVãTion

Many people who hold Tu B'Shevat seders draw on Passover for inspiration. Gathering on the evening of Tu B'Shevat or on a nearby Sunday, the celebrants prepare a seder plate of fruits and drink four cups of wine or grape juice, ranging from white (representing the midst of winter) to deep red (representing the full blossoming of spring). Then they tell the story of the trees.

Creating their own Four Questions, they might ask, "On all other days, we eat only one or two kinds of fruits. Why on this day do we eat seven? On all other days, we eat fruits from all over the world. Why on this day do we eat only fruits from Israel?"

Borrowing from the Passover song *Dayeinu,* some people offer their thanks to God for trees by saying, "If You had only given us trees for shade and not for fruit, *dayeinu*—it would have been enough. If You had only given us trees for fruit and not for fresh air, *dayeinu*. . . . If You had only given us trees for fresh air and not for building, *dayeinu*."

Through our prayers and actions we can help safeguard the natural wonders of Creation.

The lessons of Tu B'Shevat continue to speak to us. Israel is our homeland; as we build her, so she builds us. We must treat the earth with respect; it is on loan to us from God and from our children who are meant to inherit it. If we are good to the land, the land will be good to us.

HONORING AND CREATING JEWISH TRADITION

- What do you think is the most important message or lesson of Tu B'Shevat? Describe one way this teaching can help you become your best self.

  _____

  _____

  _____

  _____

- Describe a traditional Tu B'Shevat ritual or custom that you think is particularly meaningful, and explain why you find meaning in it.

  _____

  _____

  _____

- How can you add beauty and meaning to the holiday through the tradition of _hiddur mitzvah_?

  _____

  _____

- Describe a new ritual (or an innovation to a familiar ritual) that you would like to add to the traditions of Tu B'Shevat. Explain why this addition would be appropriate and how it would add meaning or beauty to the holiday.

  _____

  _____

  _____

  _____

  _____

"Botanicals," wall hanging
by Sheila Groman

CHAPTER 11

PURIM
Of Masks and Miracles

פּוּרִים

14 Adar

*And the month was turned from sorrow
to gladness, from mourning to joy.*

—The Scroll of Esther 9:22

*On Purim young
and old are invited
to dress up in
costume, feast on
holiday foods, and
share in the good
humor of the day.*

any people, some of whom are very learned, believe the story of Purim is a fantasy. They think that the events in the Book of Esther never happened and that the characters never existed (except for a king named Aḥashverosh)—no beauty contest, no lots, no gallows; no Vashti, Esther, Mordecai, or even Haman.

This might sound shocking, even disrespectful. But if you think about it, you may decide that it makes the story of Purim even more special and important. For why would such a tale be told? What lesson could it have been meant to teach? And, of all the thousands of tales that were told over time, why did the Jewish people make this tale a part of the Bible?

History or fiction, the Scroll of Esther is a serious story about bravery, sacrifice, luck, and hope, a story about believing in ourselves no matter what. It is also a story about our desire to be royalty, to be admired for our physical beauty as well as for our wisdom, to save those we love, to command loyalty, to wipe out evil, to throw ourselves into danger and emerge victorious, and to be honored as heroes.

Mordecai and Esther—the heroes of the tale—become the faces and hearts of all the Jewish people. Their story, found in *Megillat Esther* (the Scroll of Esther), helps us believe that we can be imporant and make a difference.

The Story of Purim

The plot begins after seven days of drinking and feasting, when Aḥashverosh, king of Persia, invites his queen, Vashti, to parade her beauty in front of his drunken companions. A woman of courage, she refuses and is banished as punishment. Now lonely, Aḥashverosh searches the land for a new queen. After months of "interviewing," he chooses a beautiful young woman named Esther. What he doesn't know is that Esther is Jewish.

Meanwhile, Esther's uncle Mordecai has enraged Haman, the king's chief adviser, because Mordecai would not bow down before him. Haman receives permission from the king to decree that on the 13th of Adar the people of Persia should rise up against the Jews and kill them all.

When the royal decree is made public, Mordecai tells Esther that she can no longer hide the fact that she is a Jew and that she must petition the king for the safety of the Jews. Esther replies that she cannot appear before the king unless he calls for her; otherwise, she can be put to death. Mordecai tells Esther that no matter what the risk, she must go to the king—uninvited, if necessary. So Esther fasts for three days and calls on all the Jews to fast with her. Then she presents herself before the king.

A megillah is much smaller than a Torah scroll and has one, not two, rollers. A yad—or hand—is the pointer used when reading a megillah or Torah scroll.

Haman, meanwhile, impatient for the 13th of Adar to arrive, builds a gallows upon which to hang Mordecai.

The king is not angered by Esther's sudden appearance in his court. In fact, he is delighted to see her and offers to grant her most extravagant wish. Esther does not tell the king about Haman's plan right away. Instead, she invites the king and Haman to a dinner, and after the meal she invites them to a second dinner. It is only at this second meal that Esther reveals herself as a Jew and accuses Haman of wanting to kill her and all her people.

Back to the Sources

Each year, on Purim we read these words:

וַתֹּאמֶר אֶסְתֵּר לְהָשִׁיב אֶל־מָרְדֳּכָי: לֵךְ כְּנוֹס
אֶת־כָּל־הַיְּהוּדִים הַנִּמְצְאִים בְּשׁוּשָׁן וְצוּמוּ עָלַי
וְאַל־תֹּאכְלוּ וְאַל־תִּשְׁתּוּ שְׁלֹשֶׁת יָמִים לַיְלָה
וָיוֹם גַּם־אֲנִי וְנַעֲרֹתַי אָצוּם כֵּן וּבְכֵן אָבוֹא
אֶל־הַמֶּלֶךְ אֲשֶׁר לֹא־כַדָּת וְכַאֲשֶׁר אָבַדְתִּי אָבָדְתִּי:

And Esther sent word to Mordecai: "Go and assemble the Jews of Shushan and fast on my behalf. Do not eat or drink for three days. I and my maidens will fast too. Then I shall go to the king, though it is against the law. And if I perish, I perish." (Esther 4:15–16)

In remembrance of Esther's bravery and the solidarity of the Jewish people, we fast for one day (from daylight to darkness) on the 13th of Adar.

Esther accusing Haman

The king is furious and orders his men to hang Haman immediately on the very gallows that Haman has built for Mordecai. That is the end of Haman. But even the king cannot annul a royal decree. So he does the next best thing and issues a second decree, permitting the Jews to defend themselves against those who rise up against them.

The Persians react with shock and fear. Many become Jews, "for the fear of the Jews had fallen upon them" (Esther 8:17), while others support them: "Many princes and governors and those who did the king's business helped the Jews" (Esther 9:3). But although many others cannot resist the royal decree that permitted them to try to kill the Jews, the Jews successfully defend themselves on the 13th of Adar and celebrate their victory on the 14th of Adar. That is the day that has become Purim. The Jews of the walled city of Shushan fought on the 13th and 14th of the month and celebrated on the 15th. That is why today Jews in Jerusalem and other once-walled cities celebrate Purim on the 15th of Adar.

A Book of Faith
Though it never mentions God, *Megillat Esther* is a book filled with faith. Faith that good will win out over evil. Faith that we can and must take a lead in shaping our destiny. And faith that we will not be overwhelmed by greed and evil.

What Do You Think?

Purim are "lots," numbers that are picked at random, as in a lottery. The holiday's name comes from the way Haman chose the day on which the Jews were to die. It implies that the Jews' future was left to chance.

If you could give Purim another name, what would it be? Why would it be a good name for the holiday?

_____

_____

_____

How We Celebrate

On Purim as on other holidays, we share our joy with others. Many Jews assemble *mishloah-manot*—elaborate baskets of fruits, pastries, and candy—to give away to neighbors, friends, and people at school and at work. Decorated bags with little gift cards attached make perfect *mishloah-manot* containers; so do paper bags decorated with stickers and ribbons. Most *mishloah-manot* contain some form of hamantashen, which are three-cornered, fruit-filled pastries. Nuts, dried fruits, apples, oranges, and candy round out the menu.

Baking hamantashen

ONE PEOPLE, MANY CUSTOMS:
Mishloaḥ-Manot Drives

Today, some synagogues and schools organize *mishloaḥ-manot* drives. Such drives help busy people send packages they might not otherwise have time for, limit waste (what do you do with so much food?), and raise money for the synagogue or school.

A list of members is distributed and a fee for sending each package is set. Participants select the names of those to whom they want to send a package, and one package is sent to each recipient, with a list of names of all the people who joined in sending it.

Light Bulbs: Sharing Your Bright Ideas

Imagine that you are a member of a synagogue committee that is organizing a *mishloah-manot* drive. Draft a letter to the members of your congregation that explains what the plan is, why it is a good way to celebrate the holiday, to what cause the money that is raised will be donated, and how they can participate.

_____

_____

_____

_____

_____

_____

_____

_____

_____

_____

_____

_____

_____

_____

_____

_____

_____

_____

In addition to giving *mishloah-manot*, we also give tzedakah (*matanot la'evyonim,* gifts to the poor) to help make Purim a happier day for everyone.

We go to the synagogue on Purim to hear the reading of *Megillat Esther*. We hear it read in the evening and in the morning. But we don't just listen. We cheer with it and yell at it. Some *Megillah* readers use different voices to act out the roles of the characters. Most synagogues use noisemakers—called *graggers* or *ra'ashanim*—to drown out Haman's name whenever it is read. A variation on *graggers* is to write Haman's name on the soles of your shoes and stamp your feet each time his name is mentioned until his name is rubbed out. Some services even have prompters to help the congregants catch the name should they miss it and then to quiet them so that the reading can continue.

TAKING ACTION: TZEDEK

Purim is a joyous time, a time when we celebrate because justice—*tzedek*—was done, the Jews of Persia were saved, and Haman was punished. Our tradition teaches that God needs us as partners in the Covenant to ensure that not only we, but that all people are treated with justice.

There are times when it is difficult to stand up for what is fair and right—when it is difficult to speak out against prejudice and intolerance. But we should remember that Esther came to the aid of her people even though it meant risking her own life. We have always needed, and we will always need, Esthers and Mordecais.

For one week, follow the national or international news reports in a newspaper, online, on television, or on the radio. Pay attention to situations in which there is human suffering, such as reports of natural disasters, wars, or acts of prejudice. Then brainstorm actions you can take to help relieve the suffering. Perhaps you can write to your representative in Congress, stating your concern; maybe you can locate organizations that are collecting money or holding rallies on behalf of the people who are suffering. Outline your action plan, and then take action!

_____

_____

_____

_____

_____

_____

_____

_____

The Torah instructs us: "Justice, justice shall you pursue" (Deuteronomy 16:20). So stretch your heart, your body, and your shoes and get ready to take actions that will help make the world a more just place.

A Tradition of iNNoVãTion

In 2001, Ma'yan: The Jewish Women's Project of the JCC in Manhattan invited more than 200 artists to design a new ritual object—a flag—to honor the brave women of Purim: Esther and Vashti. The goal was to enrich the holiday by creating a new custom of waving a holiday flag when Esther and Vashti's names are mentioned during the holiday reading of *Megillat Esther*. Ma'yan asked the artists to design flags that would make a joyous sound as they are waved, in contrast to the harsh noise of a *gragger*.

Use this space to draw a flag that honors Esther and Vashti.

This Vashti-Esther Jester Flag was created by Melissa Dinwiddie. The artist used silk ribbon, a gilded wooden dowel, crystal beads, a gel pen, and metallic thread to make the flag.

On Purim, as on Ḥanukkah, there are no work restrictions. But toward the end of the day, families and friends gather for a festive meal, a *se'udah.* They may write funny poems or stories or even a funny Kiddush. Almost nothing is too outrageous on this day.

And of course we eat hamantashen, filled with jelly, prunes, poppy seeds (*muhn*), or even chocolate. Other names for hamantashen are Haman's pockets and *oznei Haman* (Haman's ears). Hamantashen can be bought in some bakeries, but it is also great fun to make them.

Most synagogues also hold carnivals and costume parades on Purim or on a Sunday close by. Sometimes even the rabbis dress up.

Despite the laughter and the joy of the Purim celebration, we hope and pray that there will be no new Purims for the Jewish people.

Many schools put on plays that retell the story of Purim. Some schools and synagogues also put on Purim shpiels, humorous shows that poke fun at their teachers and leaders —all in the spirit of love and good humor, of course.

HONORING AND CREATING JEWISH TRADITION

- What do you think is the most important message or lesson of Purim? Describe one way this teaching can help you become your best self.

  _____

  _____

  _____

  _____

- Describe a traditional Purim ritual or custom that you think is particularly meaningful, and explain why you find meaning in it.

  _____

  _____

  _____

- How can you add beauty and meaning to the holiday through the tradition of *hiddur mitzvah*?

  _____

  _____

- Describe a new ritual (or an innovation to a familiar ritual) that you would like to add to the traditions of Purim. Explain why this addition would be appropriate and how it would add meaning or beauty to the holiday.

  _____

  _____

  _____

  _____

This tapestry, by Naomi Hordes, illustrates the story of how our matriarch Sarah observed the mitzvah of hachnasat orhim—*hospitality—by baking bread as her husband, Abraham, hosted their three guests. The biblical quote is from Genesis 18:6.*

On Purim we observe hachnasat orhim *by inviting guests to a special meal called a* se'udah.

CHAPTER 12

פֶּסַח

PASSOVER
Retelling Our Story of Freedom

15–21/22 Nisan

*"God took us out of Egypt with a strong hand
and an outstretched arm, with awesome power,
with signs and with wonders."*

—Deuteronomy 26:8

*The many symbolic foods
and rituals of Passover
help us imagine that we
personally were delivered
from slavery in the Land
of Egypt.*

Every year at the Passover seder, Jews around the world read the Haggadah, the story of how we were delivered from slavery more than 3,500 years ago. We eat bitter herbs and greens dipped in salt water to remind us of the pain we suffered and the tears we wept when we were slaves in ancient Egypt. We recline comfortably in our chairs, thankful that we are now a free people, free to follow in God's ways and to help make the dream of a just and peaceful world come true.

Why do you think this holiday has such an unusual and elaborate set of rituals—so many foods to be eaten; four cups of wine instead of one; a special book that tells the story of the holiday; three matzot instead of two ḥallot; and four questions that we ask year after year?

Retracing the Road to Freedom

We do these things because we don't so much *celebrate* Passover as *experience* it. At the seder—a ritual meal following a specific order—we tell the story of the Exodus and relive our people's journey from enslavement to liberation. Our guide for the evening is the Haggadah.

The Haggadah is almost a script, suggesting what we should say, how we may sit, and what we can eat. But the Haggadah also invites us to share our own experiences and thoughts, declaring: "Whoever expands upon the telling of the story is to be praised."

So it is today that families often add to the seder their own creative ways of telling the story. Some even develop their own Haggadot (plural of Haggadah). These new Haggadot expand on the lessons and readings found in the original tale: a reading of the plagues might be followed by a roll call of contemporary environmental problems, such as smog or forest fires; our ancestors' struggle for freedom might become a jumping-off point for a discussion of oppression or injustice in our own day.

By speaking the story of the Exodus in our own words, we become the ancient Israelites. We recall what it feels like to be oppressed and forgotten. The Haggadah tells us that is what is supposed to happen: "Each of us should imagine that we personally went out from the Land of Egypt." In doing so, we are reminded that as God delivered us personally from the oppression of slavery, now we must work as God's partners to help liberate others.

For the Jews, freedom is just the beginning, not the goal. The goal is to serve God *willingly* instead of Pharaoh *forcibly*. When Moses first appeared before Pharaoh to ask for the freedom of the Israelites, he said, "Thus said Adonai: 'Let My people go so that they may worship Me in the desert'" (Exodus 5:1).

The Story of Our Enslavement and Liberation

The Torah tells the story of how Pharaoh set cruel taskmasters over our ancestors and of how God, hearing our ancestors cry out, commanded Moses to tell them, "God will free you."

Then Moses spoke in God's name to Pharaoh: "Let My people go so that they may serve Me." But Pharaoh would not let the Israelites leave.

The Torah tells us that God set ten plagues upon the Egyptian people. Overwhelmed by these punishments, Pharaoh permitted the Israelites to go. But no sooner had they left than Pharaoh commanded his officers to bring them back.

Encamped near the Sea of Reeds, the Israelites were terrified by the unexpected sight of the Egyptians. The Torah tells us that God then sent a strong wind that split the sea in two. A dry path formed across the bottom, and on each side stood a wall of water. Quickly, the Israelites moved across the path. The Egyptians tried to follow but the walls of water came rushing together, drowning them.

Moses and the Israelites sang a song of praise to God for protecting them; and Miriam, Moses' sister, led the women in a dance of celebration. With a mighty hand and an outstretched arm, God brought our people to safety and freedom.

Lydie Egosi has enriched the Passover tradition with her tapestry of Moses crossing the Sea of Reeds. This work and her many other Judaic textiles provide modern interpretations of Torah and Jewish tradition.

One way to personalize and enliven a seder is by singing portions of the Haggadah text, for example, "The Four Questions," the blessing over wine, and Dayeinu. You might even make up your own tunes.

Next to portions of the Bible, the traditional Haggadah is the oldest Jewish ritual text in continual use. Although 2,000 years have passed, much of the text is read as it was recited ages ago. Over the centuries, literally thousands of different Haggadot have been printed. Perhaps because the seder is based in the home, perhaps because we are invited to add our own stories and questions, many families create their own Haggadot, combining traditional passages and rituals with original ones.

If you are helping to organize a seder, you may want to suggest ways to enrich it. For example, your family might invite each guest to bring readings or personal stories on a related theme, such as immigrating to a land of freedom. Then, set some time aside during the seder to share them. Or you might invite your guests to bring their favorite Haggadot so that you can compare commentaries and texts. As with most things in life, the more you prepare, the more you enjoy.

Brainstorm four or five suggestions for enriching and personalizing your family's seder service.

_____

_____

_____

_____

_____

_____

What Do You Think?

Slavery is not always imposed from the outside. Sometimes we can be our own worst Pharaoh. Sometimes we can be oppressed by a self-pity or self-centeredness that does not allow us to see the needs and goodness of others. And sometimes we can be enslaved by a poor self-image that does not permit us to appreciate ourselves. Passover encourages us to liberate ourselves from such oppression.

Do you think that Passover is an appropriate time to seek freedom from the oppression we impose on ourselves? Why or why not?

_____

_____

_____

_____

On Passover we remember not only the pain of our own suffering but also the suffering of others. As God heard the cries of the Israelites and responded with compassion, or *raḥmanut*, so we too can pay attention to the needs of people around us. As God showed *raḥmanut* by delivering the children of Israel from slavery, so we too can help those who are oppressed.

How can you show *raḥmanut* when someone you know is unhappy, overworked, or sick?

_____

_____

_____

_____

How can you follow in God's compassionate ways when you learn of strangers who are oppressed by poverty or homelessness?

_____

_____

_____

_____

This sign greeted participants in an Avon three-day walk to raise money for breast cancer research. Many of the participants gained a new appreciation of their ability to be caring and giving and to persist even when faced with difficulties. What can you learn about yourself through the actions you take?

How Our Ancestors Celebrated

The Torah tells us how the Jews of old celebrated. Long ago, when the Holy Temple still stood in Jerusalem, the Jews were commanded to go there and sacrifice a lamb. This was done to remind them of the lamb's blood that the Israelites put on their doors in Egypt, a sign that God should pass over their houses and not kill their firstborn sons when the tenth plague came down upon the Egyptians. Then they roasted the lamb, prepared matzot (plural of matzah) and bitter herbs, and sat down to eat together and retell the story of Passover.

Passover—*Pesaḥ* in Hebrew—has always been celebrated in a family setting. Even in biblical times, if a family could not afford or eat a whole lamb, they would join with another family to eat the meal and tell the story.

After the Temple was destroyed, the ancient rabbis decreed that each family should observe Passover at home. The major symbol of Passover shifted from the Temple sacrifice to the matzah—the flat, unleavened bread that reminds us of the haste with which the Israelites prepared to leave Egypt.

How We Celebrate

Freeing Our Homes of Ḥametz

The preparation for Passover begins weeks before the first seder. Traditionally, every room in which food could have been eaten, including bedrooms and playrooms, is thoroughly cleaned. Sofas are moved, cushions are lifted, shelves are dusted. Then, in the days just before Passover, the kitchen is scoured and scrubbed. In many homes, the regular dishes and utensils are packed up and put away, and special *Pesaḥ* dishes and utensils are brought out from storage.

Why do we clean so thoroughly? According to the Bible, we are not supposed to eat anything during Passover that contains *ḥametz* (leavening). The rabbis tell us that we are not to possess *anything* containing *ḥametz*. So we clean the whole house. We remove *all* the *ḥametz*—cereal and crackers, leftover bites of doughnuts and bagels, pizzas and pretzels. Whether packaged or not, those foods must go.

What's in a Name?

Names for Passover include *Ḥag Ha'aviv,* Holiday of Springtime (symbolized by the greens on the seder plate); *Z'man Ḥeruteinu,* Season of Our Liberation; and *Ḥag Hamatzot,* Holiday of Matzot.

If you could give Passover another name, what would it be? Why do you think it would be a good name for the holiday?

_____

_____

_____

_____

The night before Passover, final preparations are made. The house is now as clean as it will be; the *ḥametz* has been removed and the Passover food has been bought. Still, you can never be too careful when it comes to *ḥametz*, so one last check, called *bedikat ḥametz*, is made. A member of the household hides a small piece of *ḥametz* (for example, a piece of dry cereal) in each room of the house. Then, in a darkened house, armed with candles, a feather, a wooden spoon, and a paper bag, the search crew begins its mission: to find the last remnants of *ḥametz* and gather them in the bag so that they can be burned the next morning.

Each time a piece of *ḥametz* is found, a family member uses the feather to sweep it ceremoniously onto the wooden spoon and from there to place it in the paper bag. When all the *ḥametz* is found, the bag is put aside in a safe place until morning. By approximately ten o'clock the next morning, after the last of the edible *ḥametz* is eaten or thrown out, the bag is burned with the wooden spoon in a fireplace or a safe spot outside. Unopened packages containing *ḥametz* can be either given away to the needy or stored away and sold, usually by a rabbi, to a non-Jew for the rest of the holiday.

A synagogue potluck pasta party can be a fun way to get ready for Passover. Invite everyone to clean out their freezers, refrigerators, and closets full of ḥametz *such as vegetable lasagna, linguine, frozen pizza, and bagels.*

You might think that is quite enough. But ḥametz is sly: It can hide almost anywhere. Maybe there are cookie crumbs in the pockets of your baseball jacket. Or perhaps you or another member of your family left a snack in a rarely used handbag or backpack. And who knows whether you ever found all the popcorn that slipped under and between the sofa cushions. So the rabbis suggest that we take one more precaution. They created a special declaration for us to recite that legally cancels all the ḥametz that we accidentally leave behind: "All ḥametz that is in my house, whether I have seen it or not, whether I have removed it or not, is hereby made invalid and as ownerless as the dust of the earth." Now, with that last act, the house is declared clean.

To be certain that all their Passover foods are free of ḥametz, many Jews buy only those foods that are marked "Kosher for Passover." (Even matzah must be labeled "Kosher for Passover" because matzah made during other times of the year does not have to conform to the regulations for Pesaḥ.)

A Tradition of Giving: Ma'ot Ḥittin

One way to clean the house of *hametz* is to throw things out. But often that is wasteful. Another way is to eat all the *hametz* before the holiday. But that can be a burden, not to mention fattening. So right after Purim, some families begin to limit their purchase of foods that are considered *hametz*. Others throw pasta parties. But perhaps the best way to clean out the stock of *hametz* is to give it away to the needy, either through a Jewish federation or a neighborhood food pantry. Some synagogues and Hebrew schools arrange food collections and donate the goods to a hunger drive.

That is a variation of an old tradition, *ma'ot ḥittin*, meaning "money for wheat." Begun in Talmudic times, it was a tzedakah campaign conducted on the eve of Pesaḥ and designed to provide the very poor with enough flour to make matzah, enough wine for the four cups, and enough food for them to enjoy a seder. For Passover is not just a *story* about freedom but an *experience* of freedom. And how can a people experience freedom if they are enslaved by hunger?

What is the difference between feeling proud of yourself—your talents, appearance, character, and personality—and having a swollen ego?

The Seder Plate

With the *ḥametz* removed, it is time to get ready for the seder. The meal must be prepared; the table must be set; the matzah, seder plate, salt water, wine, and Haggadot must be put out. Pillows, the symbol of reclining and freedom, are to be placed at the leader's chair and perhaps at the other chairs around the table as well.

On the seder plate are five ritual foods:

- *Zeroa*—The roasted bone, commonly a shank bone, symbolizes the sacrifice that the Israelites brought to the Temple and ate at their evening meal. Some vegetarians substitute a roasted beet or other elongated root vegetable for the roasted bone.

- *Beitzah*—The roasted egg symbolizes the sacrifice that was offered at every pilgrimage holiday. Many people hardboil the egg, then hold a burning match just under it to darken it.
- *Ḥaroset*—The mixture of chopped or mashed fruits and nuts reminds us of the mortar with which our ancestors built the storage cities of Pithom and Raamses.
- *Karpas*—Greens such as parsley, lettuce, or celery, or a boiled or baked potato, remind us of the freshness of spring.
- *Maror*—Bitter herbs, usually horseradish, remind us of the bitterness of our ancestors' lives. Some seder plates also include *ḥazeret,* an additional bitter herb, often romaine lettuce.

Some seder plates have a place for salt water, to remind us of our ancestors' tears.

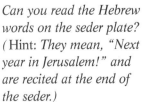

*Can you read the Hebrew words on the seder plate? (*Hint: *They mean, "Next year in Jerusalem!" and are recited at the end of the seder.)*

Other symbolic foods may also be placed on the seder table. For example, the pomegranate's many seeds can symbolize the diversity of the Jewish people and of all humankind. It can remind us that despite our differences, all people deserve a place of dignity in our community.

Imagine that you are a member of a committee that is organizing a communal seder at your synagogue. Plan on adding two symbolic foods to the seder table. Describe the foods and what they symbolize, and write a blessing to be recited before eating each one.

_____

_____

_____

_____

_____

_____

_____

_____

_____

_____

_____

Iranian Jews put a plate of scallions on the seder table as a reminder of the Egyptian taskmasters' whips.

We fill our cups to the brim to express our joy and gratitude.

The Seder

The table is set. The wine or grape juice is poured. The food is warming. The family gathers. The seder begins. As we do on most holidays, we open with the Kiddush. With that prayer, we thank God for giving us the holidays as a gesture of love and remembrance.

After the Kiddush, the greens—*karpas*—are eaten as an appetizer, but not in the usual way. The Haggadah instructs us to first wash our hands as the rabbis of old did: by pouring water from a cup or pitcher twice over each hand, this time without reciting a blessing. (Later in the seder, when we wash our hands again, we will say a blessing.) We dip the greens, which remind us of the promise of spring, into salt water, which reminds us of the tears of the Jews.

Then comes the part that children watch most intently: *yaḥatz*, the taking and breaking into two of the middle matzah. (Three

The three ritual matzot are placed separately in the three sections of a matzah cover.

matzot are set out on the seder table.) The smaller piece is returned to the plate. The larger piece is set aside for the *afikoman* and hidden. The *afikoman,* a word that some scholars think means "dessert," is the last thing we eat at the seder; the meal cannot be completed without it. So it is the time-honored tradition of adults to hide the *afikoman;* for children to search for it, find it, and hide it themselves; and for the adults to ransom it with promises of gifts so that dessert can be eaten and the seder completed.

After the breaking of the matzah and the setting aside of the *afikoman,* the story of the seder begins with the asking of the Four Questions.

Back to the Sources

Children all over the world, in Hebrew and in dozens of other languages, sing the Four Questions:

מַה נִּשְׁתַּנָּה הַלַּיְלָה הַזֶּה מִכָּל־הַלֵּילוֹת?
שֶׁבְּכָל־הַלֵּילוֹת, אָנוּ אוֹכְלִין חָמֵץ וּמַצָּה.
הַלַּיְלָה הַזֶּה כֻּלּוֹ מַצָּה?

Why is this night different from all other nights? On all other nights, we eat either ḥametz or matzah. Why on this night do we eat only matzah?

שֶׁבְּכָל־הַלֵּילוֹת, אָנוּ אוֹכְלִין שְׁאָר
יְרָקוֹת. הַלַּיְלָה הַזֶּה מָרוֹר?

On all other nights, we eat all kinds of vegetables. Why on this night do we eat only bitter herbs?

שֶׁבְּכָל־הַלֵּילוֹת, אֵין אָנוּ מַטְבִּילִין
אֲפִילוּ פַּעַם אֶחָת. הַלַּיְלָה הַזֶּה שְׁתֵּי
פְעָמִים?

On all other nights, we do not dip even once. Why on this night do we dip twice?

שֶׁבְּכָל־הַלֵּילוֹת, אָנוּ אוֹכְלִין בֵּין יוֹשְׁבִין
וּבֵין מְסֻבִּין. הַלַּיְלָה הַזֶּה כֻּלָּנוּ מְסֻבִּין?

On all other nights, we eat either sitting up or reclining. Why on this night do we recline?

Asking questions is another time-honored tradition. In fact, asking questions is so basic to Passover that the Talmud insists even learned people must ask one another questions. The truth is that any question you ask about the evening would be fine. "Why did we have to get all dressed up tonight?" "Why do we have so much company?" "What is all that strange stuff in the middle of the table?" All are good seder questions (even "When do we eat?") because they all provide opportunities to explain the rituals and the importance of the evening.

Whatever the questions, they should lead to the same end, the *maggid,* the telling. Next to the meal itself, the *maggid* is the longest section of the seder. During this part we retell the story of how the Israelites went down to Egypt, looking for food during the time of famine; how they were made slaves; how they remained proud; and how God saved them "with a mighty hand and an outstretched arm." The *maggid* climaxes in the celebration of freedom, so we sing the first part of Hallel, our song of freedom and joy.

ONE PEOPLE, MANY CUSTOMS:
Generous Servings of Karpas

As the discussion progresses, stomachs may start to growl. To allow plenty of time for the *maggid,* some hosts put out generous servings of *karpas*—carrots, broccoli, cauliflower, artichokes—plus raisins, nuts, and all sorts of dried fruits. Some families offer hard-boiled eggs dipped in salt water when the *karpas* is served. Many Reform Jews recite the blessing over the matzah early in the seder, as may have been the original tradition. This way, matzah can be nibbled throughout the seder.

After we finish this portion of Hallel, we drink the second cup of wine. The meal awaits. Rabbi Gamliel said that the seder is not complete without mentioning three things: *pesaḥ* (the passover sacrifice), matzah, and *maror.* So we begin the meal by speaking of those foods and by eating matzah, *maror,* and *ḥaroset.*

Most of the seder takes place before the meal. But two important parts are saved for after. One is the cup of Elijah, a ritual associated with the holiday's spirit of hope and purpose. No matter who is holding us down or what is holding us back, Passover teaches us that we can be freed from those chains. And with that freedom, we can change the world.

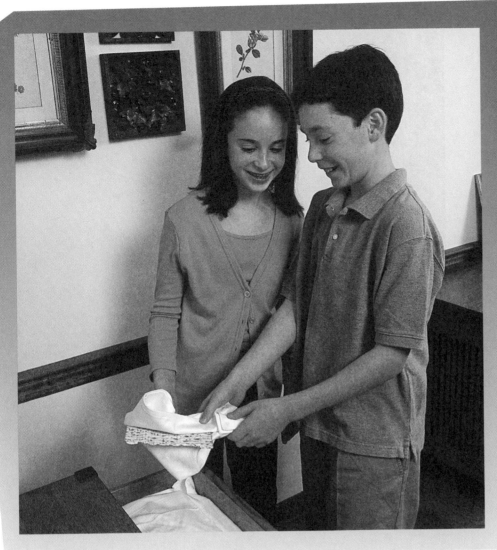

Elijah the prophet symbolizes that hope. It is thought that Elijah will one day come and settle all disputes, that he appears from time to time disguised as a stranger to help us when we are in trouble, and that he will come to announce the Messiah. At the seder, we welcome Elijah by filling a large cup with wine and opening the door for him.

Some families choose to fill Elijah's cup before the seder begins so that it can serve as a visual symbol of hope and redemption even at the beginning of the tale of oppression. Other families choose to fill Elijah's cup only after the dishes have been cleared away. Whenever you fill it, you can either pour wine directly into it from the bottle or pass the cup around, allowing all the participants to pour a bit of their wine into the cup of Elijah. This tradition symbolizes the belief that Elijah needs our help in bringing the age of redemption and that each of us can contribute our share, regardless of our age, talents, or abilities.

After dinner, the highlight of the seder is song. First we sing the remaining psalms of Hallel. Then we end the seder with songs of joy, such as Who Knows One? and *Ḥad Gadya.*

141

Today, many seder tables include a cup of Miriam. Brimming with water, the cup of Miriam is placed next to the cup of Elijah. The water represents the well that tradition teaches miraculously followed the Israelites through the desert until the day of Miriam's death.

On the second night of Passover, there is an additional ritual. No sooner does Passover come than we begin the seven-week countdown to the holiday of Shavuot, the celebration of the giving of the Torah. That sacred period is called *s'firat ha'omer,* meaning "counting of the *omer."* (*Omer* refers to the measure of grain that was brought to the Temple during those weeks.) Sometimes the countdown period is simply called either *sefirah* or the *omer.* Every night, the new day is counted as a reminder that we are yet one day closer to the ultimate purpose of our freedom: joining in the Covenant with God.

This boy is using an omer *counter. Have you ever counted the days until an important event in your life? How can counting the days to Shavuot add to the excitement of the holiday celebration?*

The period of the *omer* is a joyous time. But it is also a time of sadness, even of mourning. Tradition tells us that in Israel in the early part of the 2nd century, in the weeks between Passover and Shavuot, thousands of Rabbi Akiva's students died from a plague. Perhaps it was a plague of illness, perhaps a plague of Roman soldiers. Either way, the losses were great. To mourn these lives, many Jews today refrain from going to concerts, shaving their beards, cutting their hair, or getting married during the weeks of the *omer*.

Still, there are five days during the *omer* that are days of joy, days on which weddings may take place and celebrations may be held. Two are Rosh Ḥodesh Iyar and Rosh Ḥodesh Sivan, the first days of the months of Iyar and Sivan. The third is Lag Ba'omer, the 33rd day of the *omer*, for on that day, tradition tells us, the plague that killed so many Jews miraculously and mysteriously vanished. The fourth and fifth days, added in 1948 and 1967, respectively, are Israel's Independence Day (Yom Ha'atzma'ut) and the celebration of the reunification of Jerusalem (Yom Yerushalayim).

Many weddings, concerts, and community gatherings are planned for those days. In Israel especially, bonfires are built on Lag Ba'omer, and field days and picnics for the schoolchildren are held. Many Orthodox Jews give their three-year-old sons their first haircuts on Lag Ba'omer, and celebrate the event with a party.

ONE PEOPLE, MANY CUSTOMS:
How Many Days of Celebration?

As on the two other pilgrimage holidays, on Passover the number of days that are celebrated varies by denomination and location. Jews who live in Israel, as well as Reconstructionist and Reform Jews, celebrate the holiday for seven days, with a seder on the first night (although many choose to have a second seder, sometimes a communal one in a synagogue, on the second night). Conservative and Orthodox Jews living in the Diaspora celebrate for eight days, with seders on both the first and second nights.

This barber's cape by artist Naomi Hordes was made for a three-year-old boy's first haircut, traditionally given on Lag Ba'omer. It includes quotes from Leviticus 19:23 and Deuteronomy 20:19.

During the middle days of *Pesah, hol hamo'ed,* we can work, go to school, shop, and otherwise go about our daily lives. What we cannot do is eat or buy *hametz.* We celebrate the last day (if we are Reform or Reconstructionist) or last two days of Passover (if we are Conservative or Orthodox) by refraining from work, and we continue to avoid *hametz.*

As the last light of the holiday fades and three medium-size stars appear, the prohibition against *hametz* is lifted. The Passover dishes are carefully put away; the rabbi buys back our *hametz* and returns its ownership to us. The familiar order of the kitchen returns. We feel as though we have been away. It was fun, but it's good to be home—and free.

HONORING AND CREATING JEWISH TRADITION

- What do you think is the most important message or lesson of Passover? Describe one way this teaching can help you become your best self.

  _____

  _____

  _____

  _____

- Describe a traditional Passover ritual or custom that you think is particularly meaningful, and explain why you find meaning in it.

  _____

  _____

  _____

- How can you add beauty and meaning to the holiday through the tradition of *hiddur mitzvah*?

  _____

  _____

- Describe a new ritual (or an innovation to a familiar ritual) that you would like to add to the traditions of Passover. Explain why this addition would be appropriate and how it would add meaning or beauty to the holiday.

  _____

  _____

  _____

  _____

  _____

This wall hanging by Naomi Hordes shows Moses' sister, Miriam, rejoicing after crossing the Sea of Reeds. The Hebrew words are from Exodus 15:20–21.

CHAPTER 13

יוֹם הַשּׁוֹאָה

YOM HASHOAH
The Horror and the Heroism

27 Nisan

I believe in the sun when it is not shining.
I believe in love when I do not feel it.
I believe in God even in the silence.

—words written on a wall in a cellar used
by Jews as a hiding place somewhere in
Cologne, Germany, during World War II

Entrance to the monument in Jerusalem for Jewish children who died in the Holocaust

The Holocaust did not happen thousands of years ago in ancient times. It happened in modern times, in the middle of the 20th century. Yet like the Pharaoh of old, the new Pharaoh was determined to destroy the Jewish people.

Between 1939 and 1945, Adolf Hitler pursued two monstrous goals: the conquest of Europe and the murder of every Jew in countries under German control. At first, it appeared that he might succeed. Nation after nation caved in or joined forces with him.

Even when the Allies had evidence that Hitler was murdering Jews on an unimaginable scale, good people and good governments allowed themselves to deny it. Whether through fear or laziness, prejudice or selfishness, ordinary citizens of Germany, Poland, Romania, and other east European countries managed to live quietly next door to the horrors of mass roundups, death marches, and gas chambers. Worse yet, they often participated in the evil and became part of it.

How did those living so close to the concentration camps go to work every day, send their children to school, or celebrate birthdays and holidays while surrounded by the smoke and stench of the crematoria? How did the Nazi military and civilian death corps justify what they were doing? How did Hitler find willing executioners not only in Germany but also in Poland, Italy, France, and Greece—almost everywhere he went?

Remembering the Holocaust

Questions keep rising from the darkness of the Holocaust. Where do we draw the line between what we allow ourselves to see and what we turn a blind eye to? How much will we risk on behalf of others? Are we strong enough to withstand the onslaught of hatred? Would *we* have acted differently if we had been there?

Though Hitler failed at his goals, he inflicted a wound so horrid that it has scarred the face of humanity for all time. He not only murdered millions of Jews and other minorities. He also destroyed our faith in the natural and steady improvement of people over time. We came to understand that a world of human goodness will not happen naturally or automatically, but only with great and consistent effort on the part of each of us.

The slaughter of six million Jews, one and a half million of them children—more than all the Jews who live in the United States today—is such a staggering blow that it demands a time for remembrance and mourning. To honor the goodness and lost potential of the lives that were destroyed, to pick ourselves up, to find a way to trust the world again, to memorialize the moment in our sacred calendar—these are the tasks to which we commit ourselves on Yom Hashoah.

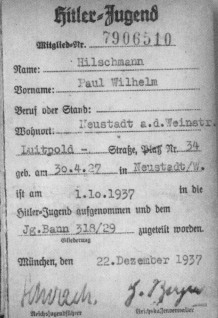

This Hitler Youth identity card was issued to Paul Wilhelm Hilschmann in 1937. So evil were the Nazis that they methodically planted hatred in the hearts of German children from the earliest ages.

The Warsaw Ghetto Uprising

Yom Hashoah is sometimes referred to as Yom Hashoah Vehagevurah, Day of the Holocaust and Heroism, for in the midst of overwhelming tragedy there were extraordinary acts of bravery.

Starved, humiliated, tortured though the Jews were, there were many instances of Jewish courage and resistance during the Holocaust. Some were heroic acts carried out by an individual, and some were sophisticated strategies implemented by the community. The largest and most famous—the Warsaw Ghetto Uprising—took place in Poland on the eve of Passover, April 19, 1943. It was the very day on which the Germans intended to deport those in the ghetto to concentration camps.

The Jews of the Warsaw Ghetto understood that their battalion of starving civilians, armed with only a few hundred guns and homemade bombs, was no match for a modern army rich in trained soldiers, machine guns, and tanks. Yet they fought with courage. It took the Nazi troops 27 days to take the ghetto, longer than it took them to overcome all of Poland. If the uprising failed to liberate the Jews of Warsaw from their oppressors, it failed with heroic glory.

On April 19, 1943, Mordecai Anielewicz led the Warsaw Ghetto Uprising. He was killed three weeks later at age 23.

Remembering the Lives

We remember the Jews who were killed in the Holocaust: parents, children, aunts, uncles, cousins, grandparents, and friends; scientists, lawyers, peddlers, rabbis, dancers, cooks, and poets. We build monuments in part to remember the horror of their deaths. But even more, we build monuments so that we will not forget the richness of their lives.

TAKING ACTION: COURAGE

Ometz lev means "courage" or "strength of heart." When we fully set our heart on doing something, our determination can give us the inner strength to overcome fear, doubt, and other obstacles in our path. Dedicating one's heart to Jewish values, such as the beliefs that all human beings are made in God's image (*b'tzelem Elohim*) and that peace and justice must be pursued, can help develop such determination.

Because we Jews so often and so brutally have been the victims of hatred, we must develop the inner determination and courage to help those who are oppressed.

To what mitzvah or Jewish value can you commit yourself to help you develop *ometz lev?* Describe two actions you can take to observe that mitzvah or value.

_____

_____

_____

_____

_____

_____

_____

_____

_____

Hannah Senesh was a woman of great courage. Born in Hungary, she left in 1939 to settle in Eretz Yisrael. *In 1942, Hannah joined a group of Jewish parachutists dedicated to fighting the Germans. She was caught in Hungary in March 1944 trying to free prisoners of war, and was executed on November 7, 1944, at age 23.*

149

In many cities, including Los Angeles, Washington, D.C., and New York, Holocaust museums have opened and are teaching visitors about the richness of the victims' lives as well as about their tragic deaths. We record oral histories with a sense of urgency, while the last generation of witnesses is still with us.

Schools throughout the United States teach about the Holocaust, reminding all Americans of the importance of tolerance, understanding, and living with one another in peace. Holocaust education is not just about what happened to the Jews. It is about how easy it is to let evil live next door; how easy it is for us to close our eyes, our ears, and our noses.

The lessons of the Holocaust are for everyone. They teach us that evil must be challenged the moment it rises, that it should

Kristallnacht: The Night of Broken Glass

Some people consider the night of November 9, 1938, to be the start of the Holocaust. On that night, thousands of Germans—encouraged and organized by their government—destroyed more than 200 synagogues, burned tens of thousands of Jewish books in town squares, ransacked more than 800 stores and homes owned by Jews, and arrested thousands of Jewish men simply because they were Jews. Today many communities hold special events to commemorate Kristallnacht and to remind us how important it is to protect freedom and democracy around the world.

This Holocaust Museum at Temple Emanu-El in Livingston, New Jersey, includes ritual objects that survived the Shoah.

be allowed no compromise because compromise only makes it want more, and that good people contribute to evil causes when they sit and do nothing.

At the dedication of the U.S. Holocaust Memorial Museum in Washington, D.C., Elie Wiesel, a Nobel Peace Prize recipient and a Holocaust survivor, said, "Indifference to evil is evil." And so it is, for evil left unchecked will flourish. Once the Nazi killing began, Hitler targeted other minorities, including Gypsies, Communists, and homosexuals. Anyone who was different was at risk.

"First they came for the Jews and I was silent," teaches Pastor Martin Niemöller, who lived in Germany during World War II, "for I was not a Jew. Then they came for the Communists, and I was silent, for I was not a Communist. Then they came for the trade unionists, and I was silent, for I was not a trade unionist. Then they came for me. But there was no one left to speak for me." After welcoming the Nazis as they rose to power, Pastor Niemöller recognized the dangers of their ways and spoke against them. As a result, he spent the war years imprisoned in Nazi concentration camps.

Righteous Gentiles

There is yet another inheritance of the Holocaust, a legacy of quiet yet extraordinary heroism. It is the legacy of the Righteous Gentiles.

In two countries, many good people, led by their heads of state in acts of civil disobedience, succeeded in defying Hitler. In order to identify who was a Jew and who was not, Hitler ordered all the Jews in all countries he controlled to wear yellow Stars of David on their clothing. He relied on non-Jews to identify all those who did not comply. That worked in many countries, but not in Holland or Denmark. When the order for Jews to wear the star was issued in Holland, 300,000 Jewish stars were sewn and worn by the country's non-Jews. Each star proclaimed, "Jews and non-Jews stand united in their struggle." It is reported that in Denmark, the law was never even ordered because King Christian X had warned that if there were such a law, he would wear a yellow star himself.

Today, as survivors of the Holocaust tell their stories, we hear more and more about the hidden children—Jewish children who were saved by Righteous Gentiles. They were either hidden in secret places, as Anne Frank was, or they were "adopted" by Christian families or convents who pretended that they were their own children. Tens of thousands of Jewish children were saved that way, even while those who cared for them risked death.

Yad Vashem is the Holocaust memorial located in Jerusalem. It includes a tree-lined path called the Avenue of the Righteous, a memorial to non-Jews who risked their lives to save Jews.

What Do You Think?

Among the many heroes of the war, two have achieved great fame. One is Raoul Wallenberg, a Swedish diplomat who saved thousands of Jews by giving them food, clothing, medicine, and false passports for safe passage in and out of Europe. He is believed to have died in a Soviet prison, a prisoner of war, without knowing that the world praises and honors him. The other is Oskar Schindler, who saved more than 800 Jews by convincing the Germans that he needed them to work in his munitions factory. Quietly, without fanfare, without fame, thousands of other Righteous Gentiles endangered their lives so that Jews could live.

List three character traits you think Righteous Gentiles had in common with one another, and explain why you think so.

_____

_____

_____

_____

_____

Describe one way you can honor the memory of Righteous Gentiles.

_____

_____

_____

How We Observe Yom Hashoah

The 27th of Nisan, five days after the last day of Passover, is the day that the State of Israel has declared to be Yom Hashoah, the day dedicated to the memory of the Jews who were killed in the Holocaust. The holiday is too young to have developed one standard ceremony or prayer acceptable to all. Still, some customs are gaining popularity.

On the evening of Yom Hashoah, many families light a yellow *yahrtzeit,* or memorial, candle in their homes to keep alive the memories of all the Jews who died in the Holocaust. Others light six, symbolizing the six million Jews who died. On college campuses, in synagogues and schools, in statehouses around the country, and in town squares and elsewhere, people gather to read aloud the names—one by one—of those who died, the towns they came from, their ages when they died.

Observing a moment of silence after lighting a yellow yahrtzeit *candle*

A Tradition of iNNoVãTion

A *yahrtzeit* is the anniversary of someone's death. In Judaism, we remember our loved ones on that anniversary. Usually families light white *yahrtzeit* candles for their loved ones. The candles are designed to burn for 25 hours, so that every moment of the day will be filled with the light of the person's memory. On Yom Hashoah, to distinguish between a personal loss and a national loss and to remind us of the yellow star the Jews were forced to wear under Hitler, many people light a yellow candle.

ONE PEOPLE, MANY CUSTOMS:

A Fast of Silence

Rabbi Michael Strassfeld suggests that to observe Yom Hashoah we should bring back the Jewish tradition of the fast of silence. Such a fast can give us the quiet to reflect on the *world's silence* in the face of Hitler's cruelty and destruction, as well as help us pray for the strength to speak out against prejudice and hatred.

What do you think would help you more to honor the memory of those who died in the Holocaust, observing a day of silence or discussing what happened in Nazi Germany? Why?

Back to the Sources

Many Yom Hashoah memorial services include the El Malei Raḥamim prayer, which opens with these comforting words:

אֵל מָלֵא רַחֲמִים, שׁוֹכֵן בַּמְּרוֹמִים, הַמְצֵא מְנוּחָה
נְכוֹנָה תַּחַת כַּנְפֵי הַשְּׁכִינָה...

Exalted, compassionate God, grant infinite rest in Your sheltering presence . . .

Light Bulbs: Sharing Your Bright Ideas

Imagine that you are a member of your synagogue's ritual committee and you have been asked to suggest a prayer, poem, or other reading to include in the Yom Hashoah memorial service. What would you want to suggest? Why?

_____

_____

_____

_____

_____

_____

Communities and schools often sponsor memorial and educational programs that include the lighting of a menorah with six branches, one branch for each million victims. Survivors, children of survivors, liberators of the camps, Righteous Gentiles, and hidden children are sometimes asked to tell their stories and are given the honor of lighting the menorah.

Members of some communities gather together and sit on the floor, as on Tisha B'Av, and read stories of the Holocaust by contemporary writers. Others read psalms and memoirs by victims of the Holocaust or diaries of those who lived through the horror.

This memorial at Yad Vashem in Jerusalem is for Janusz Korczak, a Polish Jew who was murdered by the Nazis when he refused to abandon the orphans he was caring for. On Yom Hashoah, you might honor Korczak's memory by donating tzedakah to an organization that helps children in need.

A book of recipes, written from memory by the starving women of Theresienstadt and salvaged from the fires of the war, gives us an opportunity to celebrate their lives in ways that they themselves chose. Many of the recipes are for rich, sweet cakes and desserts. A recipe chosen from that book, *In Memory's Kitchen,* can become part of a ceremony of remembrance. Friends or members of a synagogue or family can gather in the kitchen to prepare it. While it is baking, they may study Torah together, in memory of the victims and in celebration of their lives, or they may read from the diaries or the memoirs of the survivors or their children.

When the baking is done, the participants can sit at a table and with modest ceremony eat of the food that kept the hopes and the dignity of the Jews of Theresienstadt alive. The meal can be simple or elaborate, but it should be one for which the diners are seated, one at which the pace is leisurely, with plenty of food set on the table. For the memory of food in the camps is a memory of the prisoners, bowls in hand, lining up only to be told how much they could have and how long they could sit. At the meal, stories of the lives of the Jews who died, stories of Righteous Gentiles, or stories of the survivors and their children should be told. In time, perhaps a new Haggadah of memory, sadness, defiance, and celebration will evolve.

HONORING AND CREATING JEWISH TRADITION

- What do you think is the most important message or lesson of Yom Hashoah? Describe one way this teaching can help you become your best self.

  _____

  _____

  _____

  _____

- Describe a Yom Hashoah ritual or custom that you think is particularly meaningful, and explain why you find meaning in it.

  _____

  _____

  _____

- How can you add beauty and meaning to the holiday through the tradition of *hiddur mitzvah*?

  _____

  _____

- Describe a new ritual (or an innovation to a familiar ritual) that you would like to add to the traditions of Yom Hashoah. Explain why this addition would be appropriate and how it would add meaning or beauty to the holiday.

  _____

  _____

  _____

  _____

  _____

  _____

This wall hanging, "Midnight Sun" by Sheila Groman, is a tribute to the Righteous Gentiles who helped Danish Jews cross the Baltic Sea to safety in Sweden.

CHAPTER 14

יוֹם הַזִּכָּרוֹן, יוֹם הָעַצְמָאוּת, יוֹם יְרוּשָׁלַיִם

YOM HAZIKARON, YOM HA'ATZMA'UT AND YOM YERUSHALAYIM

Israel's Rebirth

4, 5, and 28 Iyar

We never lost our hope, the hope of 2,000 years, to be a free people in our own land, the land of Zion and Jerusalem

—from *Hatikvah,* the unofficial anthem of the State of Israel, by Naftali Herz Imber

When you visit Jerusalem, you can go to the Western Wall, a supporting wall of the Second Temple.

Can you imagine leaving your family and friends, and the only home you've ever known, to settle in a land thousands of miles away? How might you find the courage to make the journey if it were filled with hardship and danger? How might you meet the challenge of learning a new language, making new friends, and adjusting to a new culture and climate? What might give you the strength to keep going even when you felt discouraged or lonely?

Millions of Jews have confronted these challenges in their determination to return to the Land of Israel. Kessaye Tevajieh, an Ethiopian Jew who came to Israel in 1985, describes her difficulty in making the decision to leave Ethiopia: "I had already heard that most of the family on one side, on my mother's side . . . had died on the road. It was hard to hear this and to think about leaving my family." But just as those before her had accepted the challenge of the journey, so Kessaye continued in their footsteps. For the bond between our people and our land has never been broken.

Israel Is the Jewish Homeland

Israel is the home of our earliest ancestors, where Abraham and Sarah, Isaac and Rebecca, and Jacob, Rachel, and Leah first planted roots. It is the home of our wise men and women, such as the prophets Isaiah, Deborah, and Jeremiah, and the rulers King David and King Solomon. It is the home to which our thoughts return: Every Passover and Yom Kippur we say "Next year in Jerusalem." Every time we recite the Birkat Hamazon—or Grace After Meals—we speak of our return to Israel. We thank God for giving us "the pleasing, good, and spacious land." We ask God to be gracious to Jerusalem, for the welfare of Jerusalem determines the welfare of the Jewish people.

King Solomon built the First Temple in Jerusalem.

Back to the Sources

Three times a day for 2,000 years, Jews have faced Jerusalem and prayed to be returned to our homeland:

תְּקַע בְּשׁוֹפָר גָּדוֹל...וְקַבְּצֵנוּ יַחַד מֵאַרְבַּע כַּנְפוֹת הָאָרֶץ....

וְלִירוּשָׁלַיִם, עִירְךָ, בְּרַחֲמִים תָּשׁוּב, וְתִשְׁכּוֹן בְּתוֹכָהּ כַּאֲשֶׁר

דִּבַּרְתָּ, וּבְנֵה אוֹתָהּ בְּקָרוֹב בְּיָמֵינוּ.

Sound the great shofar . . . and gather our exiles from the four corners of the earth. . . .
Return in compassion to Jerusalem, Your city, O God; let Your presence dwell there as
You have promised. Rebuild her speedily in our day. (from the Amidah)

A Tradition of Courage and Struggle

After the destruction of the Second Temple, our ancestors carried the Torah with them out from Jerusalem to the four corners of the earth. And each succeeding generation prayed that we would once again live in the Land of Israel, *Eretz Yisrael,* as a holy people.

In the late 19th century, a group led by journalist Theodor Herzl recognized the need for a Jewish state to ensure Jewish liberty. They created a political movement dedicated to establishing such a state. Herzl and the other activists called themselves Zionists, people who believe in the right of the Jewish people to exist as a free and sovereign nation in their own land.

When the British gained control of Palestine after World War I, they attempted to accommodate the Jews who lived there. There was freedom of movement and little to no tension between the British and the Jews. However, in the 1930s and 1940s tensions arose when large numbers of European Jews escaping the oppression of Germany and the horrors of the Holocaust tried to settle in Palestine. The British, fearing trouble with the local Arabs and the surrounding Arab nations, did not want the European Jews to enter Palestine. Blockades were established and boats laden with war-weary Jews were turned away.

This tapestry by Naomi Hordes includes words from the Amidah: "May our eyes witness Your merciful return to Zion."

What Do You Think?

Eliezer Ben Yehuda (1858–1922) is known as the father of modern Hebrew. An early Zionist who was raised in Lithuania, Ben Yehuda knew that a people returning to its homeland from dozens of cultures needs a common language. Hebrew had long been a language of prayer, study, and literature. But it was no longer spoken. Ben Yehuda sought to change that. Upon arriving with his family in Jaffa in 1881, he set up the first Hebrew-speaking household since biblical times. In his tireless campaign to revive the spoken language, Ben Yehuda created the first modern Hebrew dictionary, which was completed by his wife Ḥemdah after his death.

Because of Eliezer and Ḥemdah Ben Yehuda's efforts, Jews around the world now have a common language in which to discuss everything from the Bible to soccer to computers to politics to the latest action movie. Do you think it is important that Hebrew be the language of the modern Jewish state? Why or why not?

_____

_____

_____

_____

These signs mark two streets in Jerusalem, Ben Yehuda and King George V. Each reflects an aspect of our homeland's heritage—the dedication of Zionists who helped create the modern State of Israel, and the British ruler of Palestine.

In 1947, the British decided to withdraw from Palestine, leaving the United Nations—only two years old—in charge. In an effort to keep the peace, the UN voted on November 29, 1947, to divide the territory, giving half to the Arabs and half to the Jews. Jerusalem was to be controlled by an international group. The Jews of Palestine agreed to this arrangement, but the Arab nations did not.

On May 14, 1948—the 5th of Iyar on the Jewish calendar—the day before the last British officer left, Israel declared its independence. That night the neighboring Arab nations attacked. It was a difficult and costly war. Every Jew who could hold a gun or a rock, drive a vehicle or deliver a message, became a soldier. Every piece of land given to the Jews by the partition agreement needed to be defended. The Jews were outnumbered, and many died. But they defeated the Arab nations.

Before the eyes of the world, *Medinat Yisrael,* the modern State of Israel, was born. A great miracle happened there.

The Vote

On November 29, 1947, Jews around the world gathered in front of their radios to hear the United Nations' vote on partitioning Palestine into separate Arab and Jewish states, a recommendation made by its own Commission on Palestine. The roll call began: "Afghanistan, no; Argentina, abstain; Australia, yes." Then Belgium, Belorussia, Bolivia, Brazil, Canada—all yes: the first run of affirmative votes. And so it went, country by country, 56 times. "Syria, no; Turkey, no; Ukraine, yes; Union of South Africa, yes; USSR, yes; United Kingdom, abstain; United States, yes." When the voting was done, 33 nations had voted to ratify; 13 had opposed, and 10 had abstained. The first borders of the modern State of Israel had been drawn. Today there would be dancing in homes, schools, and streets. Tomorrow, there would be war.

Imagine that you were alive on November 29, 1947, and at your synagogue listening to the United Nations' vote. Describe the atmosphere in the room and what you are thinking and feeling.

_____

_____

_____

_____

_____

_____

David Ben-Gurion reads the Declaration of Independence of the newly created State of Israel on May 14, 1948. A portrait of Theodor Herzl hangs on the wall.

How We Celebrate Yom Ha'atzma'ut

To many, Israeli independence was as miraculous as the splitting of the Sea of Reeds, the Maccabees' victory over the Syrians, and the Jews' victory over the Persians. Six hundred thousand Jews lived in Israel in 1948, the same number of households that our tradition teaches gathered at Mount Sinai after the Exodus from Egypt. Within a decade, the Jewish population had doubled. By the end of the 20th century, Israel was home to five million Jews, 700,000 of them refugees from the former Soviet Union.

Israeli Independence Day, Yom Ha'atzma'ut, falls on the 5th of Iyar. In 1949, when it was added to the calendar of Jewish holidays, Yom Ha'atzma'ut was the first new holiday in 2,000 years. Because

Many synagogues and Jewish community centers hold fairs on Yom Ha'atzma'ut. They offer a taste of Israel—selling products that are made and grown in Israel, playing Israeli music, and teaching Israeli dances.

it is so new, we are still figuring out the ways to honor and celebrate it. Some people add a prayer and psalms to the regular morning service. Some add a prayer to the evening service as well. Many say Hallel, the psalms of praise and victory recited on the pilgrimage holidays, Rosh Ḥodesh, and Ḥanukkah. Some congregations create whole services devoted to the occasion. Almost every Jewish school and community sponsors a public gathering marked with song, speeches, and dancing.

In Israel, because Jews are in the majority, the very air is filled with celebration. Schools, businesses, government offices, places of recreation—all Jewish citizens are caught up in the joy of the day. There is dancing in public squares and parades, picnics, and fireworks. The celebration comes to you. It is a national holiday, just as the Fourth of July is in the United States.

ONE PEOPLE, MANY CUSTOMS: A Yom Ha'atzma'ut Prayer Service

While there is no core prayer service that all Jews follow on Yom Ha'atzma'ut, slowly, synagogues are developing traditions and services to help them sanctify the holiday. For example Congregation Dorshei Emet, a Reconstructionist congregation in Quebec, Canada, published a service for Yom Ha'atzma'ut including a portion from the Book of Zechariah, excerpts from Israel's Declaration of Independence, and the words to "Hatikvah."

In the Diaspora, we must go to the celebration, we must develop rituals for our homes and our synagogues, and we must organize communal celebrations. For example, on Yom Ha'atzma'ut many people eat foods imported from Israel—dates, figs, oranges, nuts, and chocolates—or a meal rich with classic Israeli dishes—falafel, pita, ḥummus, and teḥinah. In honor of the holiday, many contribute tzedakah to Israeli causes, plant trees through the Jewish National Fund, or play Israeli folk or popular music.

Family members and friends can gather to make *mizraḥim*, works of art that show scenes of Jerusalem and that are hung on the eastern wall of a home or office as a reminder of the way to Zion. And in our living rooms, we can gather to read aloud Israel's Declaration of Independence.

The colors of Israel aren't just the blue and white of its flag. They're the red of Haifa's wild poppies, the green of Ein Gedi's oasis, the orange of Jaffa's orchards, and the rainbow of colors that appear in Israel's cultural, religious, and daily life.

Israel is the perfect place to find a Hebrew tutor that's right for you and your computer!

Looking for an oldie but goodie or an action movie? Check out the malls of Israel.

Although the Habimah Theater in Tel Aviv presents plays from around the world, every production is performed in Hebrew.

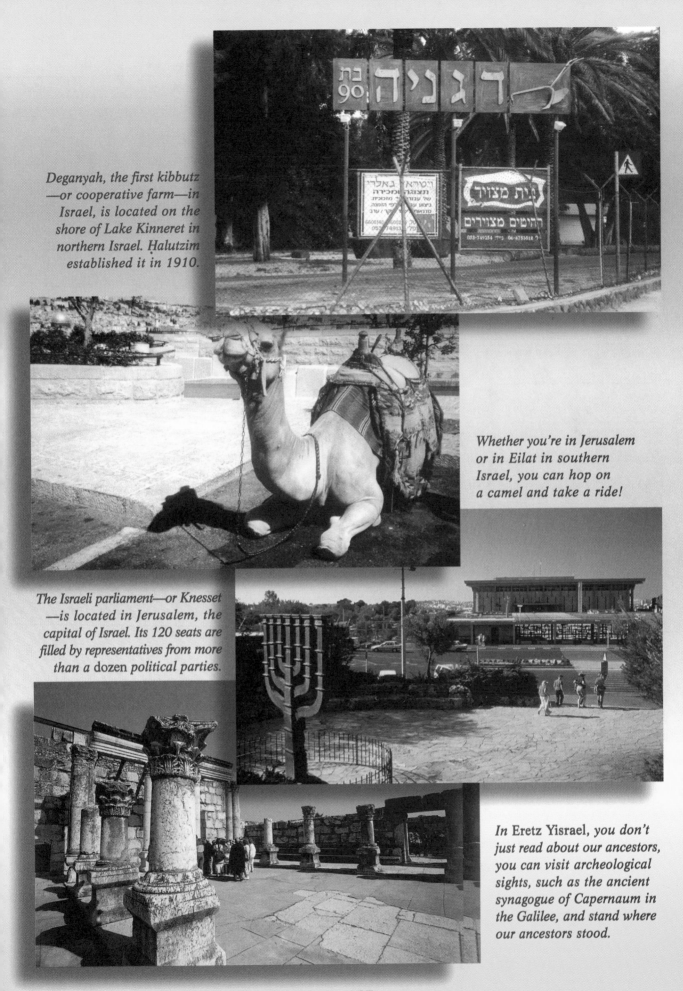

Deganyah, the first kibbutz —or cooperative farm—in Israel, is located on the shore of Lake Kinneret in northern Israel. Ḥalutzim established it in 1910.

Whether you're in Jerusalem or in Eilat in southern Israel, you can hop on a camel and take a ride!

The Israeli parliament—or Knesset —is located in Jerusalem, the capital of Israel. Its 120 seats are filled by representatives from more than a dozen political parties.

In Eretz Yisrael, you don't just read about our ancestors, you can visit archeological sights, such as the ancient synagogue of Capernaum in the Galilee, and stand where our ancestors stood.

TAKING ACTION: LOVE OF ISRAEL

From ancient times, the sages taught that it is a mitzvah, a sacred act or commandment, to love the Land of Israel. This mitzvah is called *ahavat Tziyon*—love of Zion.

We show our dedication to Israel in many ways. We visit, donate tzedakah, celebrate Yom Ha'atzma'ut, and recite words of love for *Eretz Yisrael* in our prayers.

Describe two ways you can deepen your *ahavat Tziyon*, for example, by studying the Bible or taking a teen tour of Israel.

_____

_____

_____

_____

_____

_____

Jews of all ages express their love of Israel by visiting our homeland and by making aliyah—*settling there permanently.*

Yom Hazikaron: Memorial Day

Every year on Yom Hazikaron, the 4th of Iyar, the day before Yom Ha'atzma'ut, we recall the pain and the price of the creation of the state. We remember the pioneers, the hardships they endured, and how they built up the land from sand dunes and marshes to make it livable and welcoming to those who followed. We remember the soldiers—the men and women of the Haganah, the pre-1948 defense force—and how they defended the land, sometimes with nothing more than faith and stubbornness.

But the War of Independence was not the only time the State of Israel has had to defend itself. Every few years another war or outbreak of violence has threatened its existence: the Sinai Campaign (1956), the Six-Day War (1967), the War of Attrition (1969–1970), the Yom Kippur War (1973), the war in Lebanon (1982–1985), the Intifada (1987–1993), the Gulf War (1991), and the terrorist acts that have continued into the 21st century. So today on Yom Hazikaron, we remember not only those who fell in 1948 but also all the soldiers and the citizens of Israel who have fought and died for our homeland.

On that day in Israel, the Israeli flag is flown at half-mast, and people visit the cemeteries where their families, neighbors, and friends are buried. Hardly a family exists in that small country that has not lost a loved one to bombs or bullets. For two minutes on the morning of the 4th of Iyar, throughout the entire country, a siren is sounded. Wherever people are—on a highway, on a bus, at home, in a store, walking—they stop and stand in silence. In that one moment, every Jew throughout Israel remembers the pain of the birth and safeguarding of Israel.

Light Bulbs: Sharing Your Bright Ideas

Imagine that you are a member of a synagogue committee that plans group trips to Israel. You want to plan a teen tour for the religious school and have been asked to write a brief article for the synagogue newsletter explaining why you think such tours are important.

Use the space below to write the article. Explain how both the students and the larger synagogue community can benefit from the teens visiting Israel.

_____

_____

_____

_____

_____

_____

_____

_____

_____

A Tradition of iNNoVãTion

This modern prayer begins with traditional words that connect us to our ancestors:

May the One who blessed Abraham, Isaac, and Jacob, Sarah, Rebecca, Rachel, and Leah, bless all the soldiers of Israel, all who stand guard to defend our land and these holy cities, from the border of Lebanon to the Egyptian desert, from the Mediterranean Sea to the sands in the far distance. May God thwart the designs of those who rise against us.

God, protect and shelter our soldiers from all grief and harm, from all wounds and injury. Grant them blessing and victory in all they do. Crown them with the wreath of deliverance and the garland of victory. And let Your words be fulfilled through them: "For the Eternal One walks with you, to fight alongside you, against your enemies, to bring you victory."

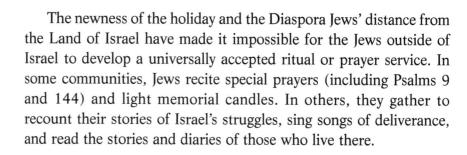

The newness of the holiday and the Diaspora Jews' distance from the Land of Israel have made it impossible for the Jews outside of Israel to develop a universally accepted ritual or prayer service. In some communities, Jews recite special prayers (including Psalms 9 and 144) and light memorial candles. In others, they gather to recount their stories of Israel's struggles, sing songs of deliverance, and read the stories and diaries of those who live there.

Yom Yerushalayim: Jerusalem Day

"If I forget you, O Jerusalem, may my right hand wither. May my tongue cleave to the roof of my mouth if I do not remember you, if I do not raise you above my highest joy" (Psalm 137:5–6). Ever since the time of King David, Jerusalem has been the earthly center of the Jewish people. Its majestic hills capture your heart. In Hebrew, you don't travel to Jerusalem, you *go up* to Jerusalem. Body and soul rise through the journey.

Yom Yerushalayim, Jerusalem Day, is the latest holiday to be added to the Jewish calendar. In 1948, when the Arabs rejected the United Nations' partition agreement, the vision of a united Jerusalem governed by international rule died. Instead, the outcome of the War of Independence decided the city's fate. When the fighting stopped, Israel had control over the modern western part of the city but not the eastern part containing the Old City and the Western Wall. That part was under Jordan's control. Jews were forbidden to go there.

THE WESTERN WALL

The Temple was a massive complex inside the walls of the city of Jerusalem. It was made up of a series of supporting walls, open courts, and inner rooms whose degrees of holiness increased the closer they stood to the innermost Holy of Holies. Of all the Temple's structures, only the Western Wall withstood the Romans' attack on Jerusalem in 70 CE. The enormous stones at the base of the wall, averaging 3¾ feet high and 10 feet long, with some as long as 12 feet, are believed to have formed the base of the wall of the First Temple, built by King Solomon almost 3,000 years ago. The wall was not part of the Temple proper but rather was part of the retaining walls surrounding the Temple.

With the collapse of the Bar Kochba rebellion in 135 CE, the last hope to recapture Jerusalem after its fall collapsed as well. Ever since, Jews around the world have turned during prayer toward the Western Wall. As an outer wall standing alone, the Western Wall represented our exile, our hopes, and our strength.

Today archaeological excavations have uncovered another site: the majestic southern approach to the Temple Mount. The grand and spacious Southern Wall has already begun to attract bar and bat mitzvah celebrations, much like the Western Wall.

The Western Wall

Jerusalem—the City of David, the City of Peace—was divided for 19 years, starting in 1948. In 1967, the Arabs once again provoked a war with Israel, hoping not just to conquer Israel but to destroy it. So began the Six-Day War. In a victory that astonished the world, Israel established herself as a formidable power; raised the spirit, image, and pride of Jews everywhere; and recaptured the Old City. The Western Wall was once again in Jewish hands and Jerusalem was united. Jews around the world stood taller after the Six-Day War.

Yom Yerushalayim is celebrated on the anniversary of Jerusalem's reunification, the 27th of Iyar. As on Yom Ha'atzma'ut, Hallel is recited in many synagogues, and in Israel many people go to the Western Wall to praise God for returning our city to us, whole.

Jerusalem is more than a city to Jews. "All the world is holy," the *midrash* tells us, "but the Land of Israel is the holiest of all. All Israel is holy, but the city of Jerusalem is the holiest of all." Jerusalem once was the meeting place of God and the Jews. Today it is the meeting place of the Jewish people. For wherever we pray, whether alone or communally in a minyan, whether with formal prayers or prayers from the heart, wherever we stand, we turn toward Jerusalem, our home, and thus toward one another.

When do you plan to visit Israel?

HONORING AND CREATING JEWISH TRADITION

- What do you think is the most important message or lesson of Yom Ha'atzma'ut, Yom Hazikaron, or Yom Yerushalayim? Describe one way this teaching can help you become your best self.

  _____

  _____

  _____

  _____

- Describe a ritual or custom associated with one of the three holidays that you think is particularly meaningful, and explain why you find meaning in it.

  _____

  _____

  _____

- How can you add beauty and meaning to one of these holidays through the tradition of *hiddur mitzvah*?

  _____

  _____

- Describe a new ritual (or an innovation to a familiar ritual) that you would like to add to the traditions of one of the holidays. Explain why this addition would be appropriate and how it would add meaning or beauty to the holiday.

  _____

  _____

  _____

  _____

  _____

This tapestry, "This Year in Jerusalem of Gold," is by Sheila Groman.

CHAPTER 15

SHAVUOT
The Greatest Gift

6/7 Sivan

When God spoke on Mount Sinai, the whole world became silent so that all the creatures might know that there is none beside God.

—Exodus Rabbah 29:9

"Shavuot" by Lydie Egosi

There are many kinds of Jews in the world. There are Diaspora Jews and Israeli Jews; Reform, Conservative, Reconstructionist, Orthodox, and secular Jews; Jews who believe in God and Jews who do not; Jews from Jewish families, and Jews from gentile families. There are generous Jews and selfish Jews; Jews who eat deli and Jews who eat Chinese food; Jews who are rich and those who are poor; rural Jews, suburban Jews, and city Jews.

With so many different kinds of Jews, what is it that keeps us together? What is it that makes us all Jews?

The answer is Torah.

The Torah belongs to all of us. It is our source of values, wisdom, and purpose. It is what Jewish life is based on. As long as we are Jews, the Torah is ours and we each have a share in it.

This Torah mantle is by Peachy Levy. In Hebrew, the five books that make up each Torah scroll are respectively known as B'reshit, Sh'mot, Vayikra, B'midbar, and D'varim (the first important word of each book). Do you know the names of the books in English?

Back to the Sources

Just as the Jewish people have been enriched by the wisdom of others, so too, many nations have been inspired by the sacred teachings of Judaism. The inscription on the Liberty Bell in Philadelphia comes from the Torah:

$$...\text{וּקְרָאתֶם דְּרוֹר בָּאָרֶץ לְכָל־יֹשְׁבֶיהָ}...$$

. . . Proclaim liberty throughout all the land, unto all the inhabitants thereof . . .
(Leviticus 25:10)

Exactly how the Torah was created, and where and when it was written down, is something we can only imagine. Were the words dictated by God to Moses on Mount Sinai? If so, how many of those words? all of them? the Ten Commandments? all but the last verses, which speak of Moses' death? Is the Torah inspired but not dictated by God? Is the Torah an anthology of our sacred tales, full of wisdom and truth but not divine?

In fact, the origins of the Torah are a mystery. Although it would be satisfying to know the source, the importance and authority of the Torah go beyond that. They are rooted in the millions of Jews who, over hundreds of generations, claimed the Torah and cherished, nurtured, and obeyed it, building from it a tradition that enriches the world. Where the Torah came from is not as important as what it means to us, how it has built our people, and where it will take us.

The Giving of the Gift

The Torah itself tells us its own story of origin. Much of the Torah was given by God to the Jews through the hands of Moses some 3,500 years ago at Mount Sinai. The story of the giving of the Torah begins when God freed the Israelites from Egypt and brought them in safety through the Sea of Reeds. God led them to a mountain, sometimes called Horeb, but most often called Sinai. It was there that God promised to come down to the mountain and speak with the Israelites. For three days, the people prepared themselves as they had been instructed.

Finally, in the words of the Torah, "on the third day, the morning dawned, and with it came thunder and lightning, and a thick cloud hung on the mountain; the voice of a shofar sounded, strong, and all the people in the camp quaked. . . . The mountain was filled with smoke because God was descending upon it" (Exodus 19:16, 18). And God spoke the words of the Ten

What Do You Think?

Although we celebrate the giving of the Torah on the holiday of Shavuot, the Torah itself belongs in the everyday life of our people. It was not meant to be the exclusive possession of the priests or of royalty. Nor were its lessons meant to be studied and observed only on holidays and special events.

Why do you think something as precious as the Torah is meant to be used so often and by so many people?

_____

_____

_____

_____

The Time of the Giving of the Torah

Some people wonder why the name *Z'man Matan Torateinu* refers only to the giving of the Torah and not to the receiving of the Torah. The traditional answer is that the Torah was given only once, years ago on Mount Sinai, whereas it is received every day. Every day each Jew receives the Torah in his or her own way and must respond based on his or her unique abilities.

A yad helps us keep our place when we read from a Torah scroll, and it protects the scroll from becoming soiled.

1. I am Adonai your God, who brought you out of Egypt.

2. Do not have other gods beside Me or pray to idols.

3. Do not use My name except for holy purposes.

4. Remember Shabbat and keep it holy.

5. Honor your father and mother.

6. Do not murder.

7. Do not commit adultery.

8. Do not steal.

9. Do not swear falsely.

10. Do not desire what belongs to your neighbor.

Commandments, beginning with "I am Adonai your God, who brought you out of the Land of Egypt. . . . Do not have other gods beside Me" (Exodus 20:2–3).

What exactly happened that day is not clear. The biblical record of events is itself fuzzy. (Read the original story, beginning with Exodus 18, and see whether you can keep track of who is where at every moment.) In a way, this is understandable, for the rabbis tell us that the Revelation of the Torah was like a wedding, a time when emotions often overwhelm memory.

How We Celebrate

All Jews celebrate Shavuot on the 6th of Sivan. Conservative and Orthodox Jews outside the Land of Israel also celebrate it on the 7th of Sivan. As one of the three pilgrimage holidays, Shavuot has both an agricultural and a historical explanation. In fact, other names for Shavuot are *Hag Hakatzir,* Holiday of the Grain Harvest; *Yom Habikkurim,* Day of the First Fruits; and *Z'man Matan Torateinu,* Time of the Giving of Our Torah.

Can you find the Hebrew name of the Ten Commandments—Aseret Hadibrot—in this picture?
Aseret Hadibrot *means "The Ten Words" or "The Ten Sayings."*

For 2,000 years, Shavuot has been celebrated as the holiday of the Giving of the Torah. Shavuot and *Matan Torah* fit together so well that the marriage seems to have been created in the Bible.

But it wasn't. Though the Torah clearly speaks of Shavuot (see Exodus 34:22 and Leviticus 23:9–22, among other places), nowhere does it link Shavuot with the giving of the Torah. In fact, it was the ancient rabbis who brought the two together. For until then, this most awe-filled moment in the history of our people had no holiday to mark it, no sacred date in our calendar on which to celebrate and relive it. And since the Torah itself tells us both that the giving of the Torah occurred in the third month after the Exodus and that Shavuot falls in the third month after Passover, the connection—once made—almost seems commanded by God.

Agriculturally, Shavuot marks the end of the spring harvest. In celebration the people of Israel would come to Jerusalem with much fanfare, bringing their harvest offerings to the Temple. Although tradition required them to bring only fruits from the seven species specifically associated with Israel, the people often brought other crops as well.

Of the three pilgrimage holidays, Shavuot has the fewest rituals. There are no required foods, no special places to sit, no things to shake or to blow. We tend to eat dairy on Shavuot (blintzes and cheesecake are popular). We light the holiday candles, recite Kiddush, set the table with two hallot, and attend synagogue services, which include the reading of special Torah and *haftarah* portions and the chanting of the Book of Ruth.

One People, Many Customs:
The Earth's Harvest

It is a tradition in some synagogues to decorate the sanctuary with greenery during Shavuot as a reminder of the bounties of fruits and grains that the pilgrims brought to Jerusalem in the time of the Temple. Some families practice that tradition in their homes as well. Boughs of lilacs and roses, sprays of baby's breath, tulips, and ferns, as well as herbs and vegetables of all kinds can fill the family room, den, dining room, and living room with their beauty and fragrance in honor of Shavuot.

In some families, it is a custom to recite Kiddush over wine made in Israel.

It is traditional to eat milk products on Shavuot. Blintzes and sour cream are a popular holiday treat.

Reading Ruth

On each pilgrimage holiday, a different *megillah*, or scroll, is read from the section of the Bible known as Writings. On Shavuot, we read the Scroll of Ruth. Ruth was a Moabite who married an Israelite who had left the Land of Israel with his family during a famine. After her husband's death, Ruth was determined to stay with her mother-in-law, Naomi, and go back with her to the Land of Israel. In joining Naomi, Ruth chose to give up her Moabite ways. Although Naomi urged her to return to her family, Ruth remained faithful, declaring, "Wherever you will go, I will go. Wherever you lodge, there I will lodge. Your people shall be my people, and your God my God. Wherever you die, I will die, and there I will be buried" (Ruth 1:16–17).

We read the Book of Ruth on Shavuot for two reasons: First, Shavuot is a harvest festival and the central events of the story take place during the harvest. And second, Shavuot celebrates the giving of the Torah. In the story, Ruth accepts the Laws of Moses and in the process converts to Judaism.

Ruth gleaning sheaves of grain in the Land of Israel

Some communities enrich Shavuot by celebrating it as the wedding anniversary of God and the Jewish people. They imagine God as the groom, the Jewish people as the bride, and the Torah as the wedding document. Some synagogues even reenact the wedding, complete with ḥuppah, or wedding canopy, and a specially worded ketubah—or Jewish wedding contract.

Many synagogues also choose Shavuot as the time for young Jews to renew their commitment to God and the Jewish people. In many synagogues, confirmation serves as a graduation ceremony from religious school or a commencement following several years of post–bar and bat mitzvah study. In other synagogues it marks a graduation to a higher level of learning. Typically, the teens give a presentation from the *bimah* in which they tell of their commitment to learning and living Torah. Through readings from the Torah and a ritual procession, they relive for us the experience of the giving of the Torah.

Our tradition teaches that every Jew is a member of the Covenant, or *Brit*, between God and the Jewish people and that the Torah belongs to us all. That is why we try to celebrate our shared traditions, respect our differences, and work as a united community—*klal Yisrael*—to honor the *Brit*.

It isn't always easy to work together. Sometimes we feel angry or impatient with one another. How can speaking respectfully about our differences help?

_____

_____

_____

_____

_____

How can studying Torah and celebrating holidays together remind us that despite our differences we are all one people?

_____

_____

_____

_____

_____

Under the Communist regime of the former Soviet Union, hundreds of thousands of Jews lived in poverty and oppression. This poster was created in the spirit of klal Yisrael *and was used to organize the New York Jewish community's participation in a 1979 rally for the Jews of the Soviet Union.*

Confirmation students can continue their Jewish education throughout high school and college. Just as we reread the Torah year after year in synagogue, so our tradition teaches us to continue our Jewish studies throughout our lives.

Imagine that you are a member of your synagogue's building committee, which is trying to raise funds to renovate the sanctuary and the religious school classrooms. Unfortunately, because of a disagreement between committee members regarding which should be renovated first, no progress has been made in raising money.

Brainstorm ideas for bringing the two sides together and reminding them of the importance of working as *klal Yisrael,* a united community.

_____

_____

_____

_____

_____

_____

_____

_____

_____

_____

_____

Create a saying or motto to help remind yourself and others of the importance of *klal Yisrael.*

_____

_____

_____

In addition, many families and synagogues observe a night of study called a *tikkun leil Shavuot.* Often, guests and congregants are invited to bring a text and a nosh, and everyone takes a turn teaching and learning. The study lasts as long as the energy and the food hold out. Some groups study until it is light enough to begin the morning prayers.

HONORING AND CREATING JEWISH TRADITION

- What do you think is the most important message or lesson of Shavuot? Describe one way this teaching can help you become your best self.

  _____

  _____

  _____

  _____

- Describe a traditional Shavuot ritual or custom that you think is particularly meaningful, and explain why you find meaning in it.

  _____

  _____

  _____

- How can you add beauty and meaning to the holiday through the tradition of _hiddur mitzvah_?

  _____

  _____

- Describe a new ritual (or an innovation to a familiar ritual) that you would like to add to the traditions of Shavuot. Explain why this addition would be appropriate and how it would add meaning or beauty to the holiday.

  _____

  _____

  _____

  _____

  _____

  _____

"Noah's Ark" by Lydie Egosi is an artistic interpretation of the text in Genesis. On Shavuot we celebrate the gift of the Torah's many sacred stories and teachings.

CHAPTER 16

תִּשְׁעָה בְּאָב

TISHA B'AV
A Time of Mourning

9 Av

How lonely sits the city that once was filled with people. . . . Our possessions have been claimed by strangers, our homes by foreigners. . . . We are orphaned. . . .

—from the Book of Lamentations

This is a model of the city of Jerusalem as it appeared in 70 CE, just before the destruction of the Second Temple. The Holy of Holies is shown at the top center.

How might you feel if your synagogue were destroyed by a flood or fire? Might you miss the time spent with your friends? Do you think that holidays and bar and bat mitzvah celebrations would be as meaningful and as much fun if everyone were forced to observe them alone, in their own homes? Would it be more difficult to organize acts of *tikkun olam*—repairing the world—for example, Yom Kippur food drives, Purim fund-raisers, and visits to the sick and elderly?

Now imagine how you might feel if *all* the synagogues—*everywhere*—were destroyed along with all the JCCs and all the Jewish schools, summer camps, and federations. Imagine what it might be like if there were no place left in the entire world where Jews could gather to pray . . . study . . . celebrate . . . and work for a better, more just and peaceful world. Might you fear that the Jewish people and tradition could not survive such a catastrophe?

Just as synagogues, JCCs, federations, camps, and religious schools are gathering places for Jews in our time, so the Holy Temple in Jerusalem was a gathering place for our ancestors. In fact, it was *the* gathering place, *the* holiest of holy places. It was so important that it was impossible to imagine the Jewish people surviving without it.

The Centrality of the Temple

For a thousand years, the Temple, or *Beit Hamikdash,* was the heart and soul of the Jewish people. Until its final destruction in 70 CE, it was in the Temple that the Jewish people gathered, bringing gifts of grain, fruits, animals, and wine to thank God for the land's bounty. It was there that they sought healing for their sick, comfort in their mourning, and celebrated the birth of a child. It was from the Temple that the leaders of Israel ruled; and it was where Jews sought the presence of God and one another's company.

Synagogues, study houses, and the family home had not yet developed as centers of religious activity. The Temple was the place where heaven and earth met. As long as the Temple stood, so the Jews thought, God stood with them. To lose the Temple was to lose more than the Jews' physical, political, and economic center. It was to lose the affection and favor of God. It was, in short, to be rejected by God.

In the year 586 BCE, the Babylonian king Nebuchadnezzar, long a foe of the Jewish nation, destroyed the Temple. He looted its treasures and forced the people into exile to Babylonia. Where once magnificent buildings had stood, only rubble and ashes remained. All was lost. There was no food, no water, no work, no government, no leaders, no hope.

TAKING ACTION: CREATING SACRED SPACE

When the First Temple was destroyed and our ancestors were driven out of Israel, they felt weakened and lonely. So they came together to read the Torah and pray to God. That is how the first synagogues came into being. Centuries later our synagogues are still places where we gather for study and prayer. When we come together as a community, we feel cared for, stronger, and less alone, and in the process of caring for one another we create holy space.

How can you help make your religious school a holy space by showing concern and kindness to your classmates and teachers?

_____

_____

_____

What can you do to make others feel welcome in your synagogue?

_____

_____

_____

Why do you think small acts of kindness, such as helping someone learn to read a prayer or find their place in a siddur, can create holy space?

What could that mean for the Covenant? Was it broken, or was it still whole and strong? The enemies of Israel thought the former; the prophets of the First Temple and the rabbis of the Second Temple, the latter. And that made all the difference.

The prophets of the exile believed that the destruction was punishment, not abandonment. For example, Isaiah wrote these words of comfort and hope from Babylonia: "Tell Jerusalem to take heart, proclaim unto her that her time of service is accomplished, her guilt paid off" (Isaiah 40:2).

And so it was. About 50 years after the destruction of the First Temple, King Cyrus of Persia defeated Babylonia and encouraged the Jews to return to Jerusalem and rebuild their Temple. The Second Temple served as the religious and spiritual center of the Jewish people for another 500 years. It stood even longer than the First Temple. The Jewish nation was reborn.

Back to the Sources

The Book of Psalms expresses our people's feelings of elation and joy upon returning to the Land of Israel.

...בְּשׁוּב יְיָ אֶת־שִׁיבַת צִיּוֹן הָיִינוּ כְּחֹלְמִים: אָז יִמָּלֵא שְׂחוֹק פִּינוּ וּלְשׁוֹנֵנוּ רִנָּה...: הַזֹּרְעִים בְּדִמְעָה בְּרִנָּה יִקְצֹרוּ:

. . . When God returned our exiles to Zion, it was like a dream. Our mouths were filled with laughter; our tongues sang with joy. . . . Those who sow in tears will reap in grateful song.
(Psalm 126:1–2, 5)

On Shabbat and festivals, it is with those words of joy that we begin the Birkat Hamazon—or Grace After Meals.

In that time, Israel occupied a strategic and highly prized position in the world because it was the land bridge between Europe, Asia, and Africa. As armies traveled through, many tried to occupy and conquer Jerusalem. Yet Jerusalem survived as Israel's capital until 70 CE, when, after a long battle with the Romans, a hard siege, and internal division, Jerusalem and the Temple were destroyed. This time, the Temple would not be rebuilt. There would be no more home for the priests and the Levites, no more sacrifices, no more psalms offered in song, no central place to go for comfort at a time of illness or loss, no sacred hearth at which to celebrate new life. The 1,000-year-old tradition of the Holy Temple would be no more.

Even in the middle of a joyous occasion, our tradition asks us to remember the sorrow of Jerusalem's destruction.

What Do You Think?

To this day, we recall the loss of the Temple and the destruction of Jerusalem of old when we break a glass at the end of a wedding ceremony. Some Jewish families and artists leave a portion of their home or their work unfinished (a corner unpainted or a molding cut short) *zecher l'ḥurban,* as a reminder of the destruction. And perhaps it reminds us as well that despite our best efforts, perfection is a goal we can pursue but never achieve. And that is OK.

Do you agree or disagree that no individual or family can be perfect, that at best we can continually strive to improve but never reach perfection? Why?

_____

_____

_____

_____

_____

And yet, as the walls of the Temple were collapsing, a remarkable drama was being played out that would secure the future of Judaism for the next 2,000 years. A rabbi named Yoḥanan ben Zakkai, tradition tells us, believing defeat was at hand, had himself placed in a coffin and smuggled out of Jerusalem. It was a trick that was intended to get him past both the Jewish zealots on the inside who guarded the gates against defectors, and the Roman soldiers on the outside who guarded the gates against escapees. Once outside, Yoḥanan ben Zakkai sought permission from the Roman leadership to set up a school in the port city of Yavneh.

The Rise of Rabbinic Judaism

The rabbis who survived the siege of Jerusalem began gathering in Yavneh. It was at that first academy that rabbinic Judaism, the Judaism of the Mishnah and the Talmud that we know today, took root. The old order was gone; a new one had to be built. And so the rabbis began building the new world on the foundation of customs and traditions that had been part of the old world.

The remains of a synagogue from the Talmudic period in Israel

The shofar, which had been blown only in the Temple, was now blown in Yavneh; the songs of praise were recited in Yavneh; the house of study replaced the Temple. Wherever a stone of the Temple fell, the Midrash tells us, there a place of study was built.

Those rabbis created the Talmud, the leading anthology of rabbinic law and lore, conversation by conversation. What began as a compilation of oral laws eventually grew into an extraordinary library of Jewish knowledge. Our Temple was no longer made of stones and metal but of black ink on parchment. God dwelt within the pages of the Talmud just as surely as God had dwelt in the Temple. Our Temple was no longer vulnerable to the bows and arrows of our enemies. It was not even vulnerable to fires. For now it was bound between the covers of a book—a big book with many volumes, a book housed in homes and synagogues across Europe and North Africa, a book that is woven into the memory of the Jewish people.

When we study the Talmud, it is as if we are listening in on the sacred conversations of our sages. When we discuss the Talmud, we add our voices to those conversations.

A Tradition of iNNoVāTion

The story is told that as Rabbi Yoḥanan ben Zakkai was leaving the remains of the burned-out city of Jerusalem, Rabbi Yehoshua walked behind him, looked at the ruins of the Temple, and said, *"Oy lanu!* What shall we do? This place that atoned for the sins of the people Israel is no more." Rabbi Yoḥanan responded, "My son, do not worry. We have another source of atonement in its stead. That is, *gemilut ḥasadim,* deeds of lovingkindness, as it is written, 'For *ḥesed,* kindness, is what I want,' says God, 'and not sacrifices'" (Hosea 6:6) (Avot de Rabbi Natan, 11a).

And so it has always been with our people—when confronted by challenges to our traditions and life, we have always found a way to adapt and enrich Judaism.

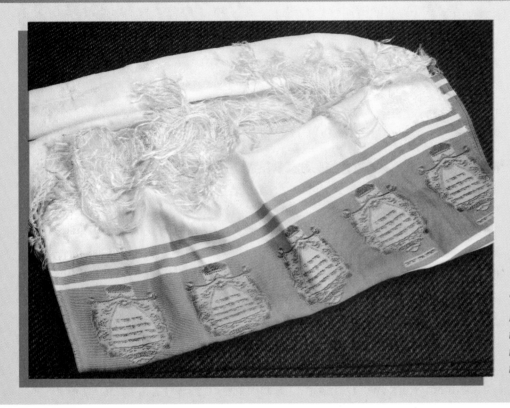

This tallit was made in Israel. Why do you think that some Jews choose to wear a prayer shawl made in Israel?

Indeed, although we Jews were exiled from the land, we were not exiled from God. For as Rabbi Shimon bar Yoḥai taught, "Come and see how precious are the Jews in the eyes of the Holy One. For wherever the Jews go in the world, the *Shechinah* [God's earthly presence] goes with them" (Megillah 29a). Although we were exiled from our physical home in Jerusalem, Jerusalem took root in our hearts. And so we face Jerusalem whenever we pray; we place Jerusalem at the top of our wedding documents; we sing of Zion at every festive meal. At the end of every seder, at the end of the long day of Yom Kippur, we declare, "Next year in Jerusalem." If we cannot live in Jerusalem, Jerusalem will live in us.

Other Days Commemorating the Loss of the Temple

Jerusalem was not destroyed all at once. A series of military setbacks (and internal disagreements) led to its collapse. Three special days recall those events. All are minor fast days, which means that their fasts last only from sunrise to nightfall on the same day:

- **Tzom Gedaliah** (the Fast of Gedaliah). On the 3rd of Tishre in 586 BCE, after the First Temple was destroyed, Gedaliah, the last Jewish governor of Judah, was assassinated by Jewish opponents.

- **10th of Tevet.** On this day the Babylonians began their siege of Jerusalem in 588 BCE.

- **17th of Tammuz.** On this day in 70 CE, the Romans broke through the city walls of Jerusalem; according to the ancient rabbis, so too did the Babylonians in 586 BCE. That was the beginning of the end. The 17th of Tammuz begins the three weeks of semi-mourning that lead up to Tisha B'Av. During that season, traditional Jews plan no weddings. Concerts and festivals are generally avoided. Wherever possible, moments that would otherwise be marked by the Sheheheyanu are postponed. From the 1st of Av until the 9th, traditional Jews serve meat and wine only on Shabbat. Liberal Jews, especially young people in Jewish camps or in Israel, focus on the observance of Tisha B'Av itself.

For 2,000 years, the holiday of exile—Tisha B'Av—has shown us how to keep hope alive, to hold on to our dreams, to never give up our will to reach the promised land. "Look, Rachel, look," a modern Zionist song says to our matriarch, "your children have returned to their land." And so we eventually did.

How We Observe the Day

Tisha B'Av, the 9th of Av, is a day of mourning. For a full 25 hours, from sundown to nightfall, we fast. It is not a fast of atonement; rather it is a fast of grieving.

On the night of Tisha B'Av, the lights of the synagogue are dimmed. Only the eternal light on the ark shines clearly, a reminder of the Temple's past glory and God's eternal presence. Congregants sit on the floor or in low chairs, one of the signs of mourning. Candles serve as the only light. The Book of Lamentations, *Eichah,* is chanted mournfully, like an ancient ballad telling a tale of love and loss. *Kinot,* poems of mourning and remembering, are sometimes sung as well. Often the ark and, occasionally, the walls are draped in black. For the 25 hours of this holiday, Jews are prohibited from wearing leather, listening to music, or bathing. Those prohibitions, too, are signs of mourning.

Tisha B'Av cannot be observed on Shabbat, for the joy of

Shabbat overrides the sadness of the destruction of the Temple. Therefore, when Tisha B'Av falls on Shabbat, it is postponed one day and observed on Sunday, the 10th of Av.

On Tisha B'Av, neither a tallit nor tefillin are worn during the morning prayer service. Both are considered symbols of joy and therefore are not in keeping with the mood. Work is permitted.

At *minhah,* the afternoon service, our spirits begin to lift. We put on tallitot and tefillin. The darkness begins to break. We read in the *haftarah* for that day, "'You shall go out with joy,' God says

ONE PEOPLE, MANY CUSTOMS:
Letters to God

Every year since the reunification of Jerusalem, thousands of Jews from all over the world have gathered at the Western Wall on Tisha B'Av to remember the Temple's glory and to celebrate the miracle of seeing Jerusalem and the Jewish nation rebuilt.

Whether on Tisha B'Av or on any other day, many people believe that God hears their prayers best when they pray at the Western Wall. It has become a tradition in modern times to write prayers on small pieces of paper and slip them into the small cracks in the huge stones of the wall. Years ago, if you could not go to the wall yourself, you would give your note to friends and ask them to place it high in the wall for you. Today technology reigns, enabling people to fax messages to the wall and to speak directly to the stones via cellular phones!

Personal prayers fill cracks and crevices of the Western Wall.

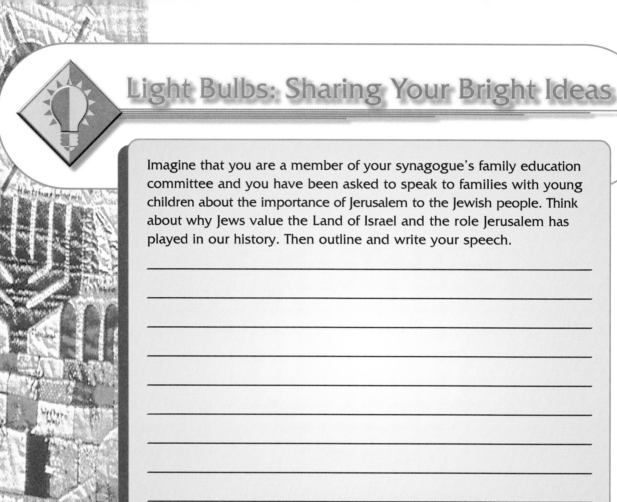

Imagine that you are a member of your synagogue's family education committee and you have been asked to speak to families with young children about the importance of Jerusalem to the Jewish people. Think about why Jews value the Land of Israel and the role Jerusalem has played in our history. Then outline and write your speech.

_____

_____

_____

_____

_____

_____

_____

_____

_____

of Israel, "and be led forth in peace. Before you the mountains and hills will break into song. All the trees of the field will clap their hands" (Isaiah 55:12). We are promised that God will restore joy to Israel. And for the generations who have lived to see the founding of the State of Israel, Jerusalem rebuilt, Jews praying at the Western Wall, and hundreds of thousands of Russian and Ethiopian Jews finding refuge in Israel, that promise has come true. Some Jews break the fast after *minḥah.*

Messages of promise and comfort continue through the *haftarot* (plural of *haftarah*) for the seven weeks after Tisha B'Av. The Shabbat immediately following the 9th of Av is called Shabbat Naḥamu, Shabbat of Comfort. Its name comes from the first words of the *haftarah,* which also strengthened the Jews of the first exile: "'Give comfort, give comfort to My people,' says your God. 'Tell her that the time of her punishment is done'" (Isaiah 40:1–2).

It is with this belief of new hope and eternal beginnings that we enter the month of Elul, listen to the sounds of the shofar, prepare for the High Holidays, and begin the cycle of time all over again.

HONORING AND CREATING JEWISH TRADITION

- What do you think is the most important message or lesson of Tisha B'Av? Describe one way this teaching can help you become your best self.

  _____
  _____
  _____
  _____

- Describe a traditional Tisha B'Av ritual or custom that you think is particularly meaningful, and explain why you find meaning in it.

  _____
  _____
  _____

- How can you add beauty and meaning to the holiday through the tradition of _hiddur mitzvah_?

  _____
  _____

- Describe a new ritual (or an innovation to a familiar ritual) that you would like to add to the traditions of Tisha B'Av. Explain why this addition would be appropriate and how it would add meaning or beauty to the holiday.

  _____
  _____
  _____
  _____
  _____
  _____

"Remember Jerusalem,"
a tapestry by Sheila Groman

INDEX